Sweet Dreams in America

Sweet Dreams in America

MAKING ETHICS

AND SPIRITUALITY

WORK

SHARON D. WELCH

Routledge   New York and London

Published in 1999 by
Routledge
29 West 35th Street
New York, NY 10001

Published in Great Britain by
Routledge
11 New Fetter Lane
London EC4P 4EE

E
184
.A1
W37
1999

Portions of this book have been previously published in somewhat different forms. The author gratefully acknowledges the following for permission to reprint. Portions of Chapter One previously appeared in *Dona Nobis Pacem: Årsbok För Kristen Humanism* (1995). Portions of Chapter One and Chapter Three previously appeared in *Studies in Christian Ethics,* Vol. 10, No. 1 (1997) and are reprinted with kind permission of the editor. Portions of Chapters Two and Four previously appeared as "Dismantling Racism" in *Theology and the Interhuman,* edited by Robert R. Williams (Trinity Press International).

Library of Congress Cataloging-in-Publication Data

Welch, Sharon D.
    Sweet dreams in America : making ethics and spirituality work /
Sharon D. Welch.
      p. cm.
    Includes bibliographical references and index.
    ISBN 0-415-91656-9 (alk. paper). — ISBN 0-415-91657-7 (pbk. : alk.
paper)
      1. Pluralism (Social sciences)—Moral and ethical aspects—United States.
2. Multiculturalism—Moral and ethical aspects—United States. 3. Social
ethics—United States. 4. Progressivism (United States politics) I. Title.
E184.A1W37   1998
305.8'00973—DC21   98-11884
                                            CIP

For my daughters, Zoe and Hannah,
my grandmothers,
Beulah Mae Lawhon and Edith Graef,
and in memory of
my parents,
James and Reta Welch

CONTENTS

ACKNOWLEDGMENTS

This work would not have been possible without the inspiration and support of my friends and colleagues at the University of Missouri, the members of the department of religious studies, the members of the women's studies program, and those people I have worked with throughout the country who are involved in diversity training and multicultural education. I am especially grateful to Mary Ellen Brown, Jaci Goldberg, Karen Touzeau, Elaine Lawless, Geta LeSeur, Mable Grimes, Carolyn Dorsey, Carol Lee Sanchez, Shirley Jordan, John McClendon, Mary Lenox, and Peggy Placier. I am grateful to Jon Poses for his care, for his expert induction into the world of jazz, and, along with Meg Riley and Lola Peters, for inspiring the title of this book.

I am also thankful for the friends who have challenged me and provided clarity and direction throughout the years: Betty DeBerg, Irma Gonzales, Susan Bruno, Mary McClintock-Fulkerson, Beth Goldberg, Charla Coleman, and Amy Shapiro. I am also indebted to Wanda Kent, Traci West, and Sheila Greenberg for their professional support and to Kris Siriwangchai for research assistance. In writing this book, I have benefited from the insightful criticisms of KC Morrison, Freda Dröes, Bob Flanagan, and faculty and students at Uppsala University and at the University of Amsterdam.

While I make no claims that they would describe their work in these terms, I have, nonetheless, seen the ethos of vitality and responsibility I describe in this book in the work of Gary Oxenhandler, Karen Touzeau, and KC Morrison, as well as in the life and work of my parents, James and Reta Welch, and my grandfather, Charley Graef.

PREFACE

In this book, I present an ethic of power, chaos, and social change informed by postmodern philosophy and liberationist political commitments. My primary aim is to describe power without resorting to either the illusions of Us against Them, or to the evasions of feminist discourses of power-with, cooperation, and consensus. To put it bluntly, I see this book as offering a model of power for baby boomers who really do have power now and are grappling with the challenges of using it well. A key dimension to this view of power is a nondualistic understanding of good and evil and, correspondingly, images of hope that can counter cynicism and despair without relying on utopian expectations or millennial dreams of inexorable progress and long-lasting social change.

Many activists in the United States are still propelled by a myth of social change similar to the comforting and illusory story of evolutionary progress. We work for justice in the hope that conditions will be better in the future; that our work, though partial, will not be in vain; that our children, that people in the future, will know more freedom, more justice, more peace.

Now, if for any number of reasons we no longer share this hope, are power and motivation still possible? I am trying to articulate, to use Michael Lerner's phrase, a "politics of meaning" that is not dependent on progress, on success, on definitively winning the struggle for justice.[1] Take, if you will, the assumption that whether society is better in the future is, quite simply, irrelevant. We cannot know if we will succeed or, even if we do succeed in some measure, if our gains will not be rolled back or left behind in the face of even greater challenges. How, then, do we work, with power and passion, for social justice without the assurances of eventual victory and without the ego- and group-building dynamics of self-righteousness and demonizing? To those of us honed on dualistic divisions of oppressors and oppressed, sold-out reformers and pure revolutionaries, it may seem that there is no fun left. What can replace the vitality of being right and on the winning side?

My aim in this book is to present a vocabulary of good, of hope, of power and chaos, contingency and change, that can sustain not just resistance but also the self-critical and creative formation of institutions and coalitions. I will develop this argument in six stages.

Stage 1. What do we do when old enemies disappear, when we win politically? What do we do when Mandela is not only released from prison but then elected president, when the revolutionary front in El Salvador is brought into negotiations, when we gain some measure of power in educational institutions, corporations, or government?

I will examine the ways in which the dynamics of critique become destructive once some measure of political power is achieved. Many of us who have had to fight our way into positions of power only feel radical when we are embattled, struggling with an enemy who clearly does not share our agenda of social justice. What happens, then, when we gain power, and say even have a measure of support from a formerly hostile administration? We may even *be* the administrators. It is often difficult to shift from radical opposition to coalition building and institutional change. When people only feel radical and alive when they are opposed, they often turn on each other to keep alive, although now in self-destructive internal power struggles, the drama and energy of the "good fight."[2]

Another dimension of the difficulties of using power well is described by Kanter's theory of proportions, her analysis of the ways in which resistance to social change increases when the "tipping point" is reached, when a sufficient number of women or people of color have decision-making positions and thus begin to exercise the power of naming: the power of naming ourselves, our identities as women, as people of color, as workers; and the power of naming the mission and operation of the organization. At this point, those who were allies in bringing in the first token representatives of other groups often become resistant, finding themselves, despite their intentions, resisting the ways in which their power is now being challenged.[3]

Utilizing Kanter's theory of proportions, I analyze in this book the enervation and in-fighting that characterizes many progressive and feminist groups. These self-destructive power struggles are fueled by simplistic understandings of good and evil, by a logic of self-righteousness and demonizing that lead us paradoxically both to evade our weaknesses (do we really know how to organize health care in the United States, do we know how to modify or replace transnational capital?) and to exaggerate the significance of mistakes, failures, and differences, taking significant differences between colleagues as a sign of fundamental enmity.

Furthermore, in the social dynamic described by Kanter, I see an inability to work with the chaos that accompanies shifts in the power of naming. While we are often comfortable with the energy and the uncertainties of the good fight, rallying the troops to oppose a clear enemy, we are not so comfortable with the chaos that accompanies changes in self and group definition.

We need cultural metaphors of power and vitality that help us move within the chaos of social change. My next step, therefore, is to describe a type of power that is as vital as that of the Right.

Stage 2. The moral vocabulary of the right wing is clear and powerful. The Right utilizes the language of certainty, questioning as immoral those liberals and progressives who have different views of what lies at the root of basic social problems. This moral vocabulary rests on sharp dichotomies— a clear delineation of us against them, of right versus wrong, of good versus evil. Note, for example, the guiding assumptions of what Jacob Heilbrunn calls the "theocrats," Catholic intellectuals who "decry relativism and cultural decadence" and advocate "the notion of a Christian nation: a nation that accepts the idea of a transcendent divine law that carries universal obligations even for nonbelievers."[4]

To many of us, the dangers of such political and moral absolutism are clear. The language of moral and political absolutes, an absolute vision of what is best for the country, and even for the world, is quite often accompanied by the phenomenon of scapegoating. Those within and without who resist or criticize the absolute end and the strategies chosen to implement it are seen as the cause of delays and defeats. Success requires eliminating and excluding those who challenge the justice of a group's vision, the coherence or viability of its strategies.

The challenge is stark: it is relatively easy to mobilize political energy under the guise of righteousness and scapegoating. Once we decide, however, to renounce the illusions and satisfactions of "Right," how do we mobilize energy for social change?

I see many activists who are well aware of the dangers of absolute vision and self-righteousness. We know the limits of our strategies for social change; we are aware of their partiality in the face of mammoth economic and political problems. For many of us, self-righteousness is no longer an option. We know that we may be wrong about too many things, and, to complicate matters even further, even when we're right, we may lose. Having the "right" analysis does not readily translate into political efficacy. So, once we lose the galvanizing power of self-righteous indignation, and therefore the authority to be in control, what next? What authorizes, sustains, legitimates, and propels risk, propels us into continued struggle, continued work for some measure of social justice?

The solution is not an abdication of power but an exercise of power that is as vital as the power of "Right," the exercise of a form of power that coexists with a deep-seated awareness of our limits and our own potential for error and harm.

I describe this power first abstractly, as exemplified in chaos theory and in understandings of the dynamics of jazz, then concretely as worked out in multicultural education and coalition politics. I present a model of engaging differences that gets us out of the evasions of tolerance—noting differences but not really taking them seriously—and the false leveling that focuses on those things we share. I criticize models of tolerance and respect in which respect means not only not judging or trying to change others, but also, that there are no grounds then, for others to seriously challenge, and perhaps even change, us. I describe in this section codes, modes of discourse through which we can engage difference in ways that are mutually challenging and dynamic. My analysis is grounded in the specific pedagogical challenges of the university (women's studies, maintaining coalitions between women's studies and black studies, multicultural education, diversity training for students, staff, and faculty) and in the work of diversity training in churches, synagogues, and businesses. The theoretical issues I raise about cultural metaphors of power, conflict, chaos, and social change are grounded in specific tensions that arise in these forms of teaching and political advocacy. I address the challenges of diversity training and multicultural education, describing the political matrix in which these endeavors play a significant role.

Stage 3. It is here, in the attempt to engage differences as we build and shape institutions, that feminist models of power are fundamentally inadequate. Feminist attempts to practice cooperation and consensus, all under the ideological grid of power-with, often evade the deep differences that exist between women.[5] I take up here bell hooks's challenge. bell hooks argues that sisterhood is not a gift but a task.[6] This task is not easy, and is often made more difficult by our adherence to the discourse of power-with and consensus. In contrast to claims that women have been socialized to be better than men at cooperation and communication, I claim that women, even feminist women, are just as bad at communication, just as bad at working together as men.

In this essay I address the failures that come primarily from internal conflicts, not primarily from opposition from external forces, not primarily from people opposed to racial justice or to the full attention to race, gender, class, and sexual orientation. My focus is on the conflicts that occur within groups that share a commitment to social justice and yet find themselves in debilitating and destructive power struggles. Why is it so hard for us to maintain coalitions? And, once we gain some measure of power (there is a grain of truth, after all, to the conservative fear of tenured radicals—some of us do have tenure, and we sometimes find ourselves as directors of programs, deans, provosts, university and college presidents), why, then, is it so hard to utilize our power within institutions to implement basic institutional change? Why do we find ourselves so often locked in conflict with each other just as we have the opportunity to transform the structures of our workplaces? Michael Lerner has written of the strange proclivity of the Left to snatch defeat from the jaws of victory—a peculiar talent that, among some circles, has been honed to a fine art.[7] Why do we defeat ourselves?

I analyze some of these gender-specific barriers to the tasks of sisterhood, of coalition politics, of communication, and of the effective use of power: the evasions of the complexity of power, the evasions of the value of conflict, the fears of exercising power oneself or seeing it exercised by other women.

Stage 4. Given the muddles we often find ourselves in when we try to use power well, what can we hope for? Can we hope actually to live out our dreams of the good, our dreams of justice and social transformation? I will next turn to a description of the good, and thus the horizon for hope, that is empowering and cannot be characterized as either utopian or tragic. Rather than a hope for eventual victory, for a world without injustice or serious conflict, I describe the power of having a more modest hope, a hope for resilience, a hope for company along the way. Rather than expect that at some time major social problems will be solved and not replaced by other challenges, I discuss what it means to hope for resilience in the face of ongoing and new challenges. I explore the paradox that seemingly lowered expectations for social change provide staying power and effectiveness. Not only are these expectations not millennial, but they cannot even be characterized as hope for an American decade, much less a century.

What is the meaning now of the American dream, no longer innocent, no longer triumphant, no longer even sure of the term "American"? Our world has changed. Ann Douglas, writing of the 1920s, "the decade ... when America seized the economic and cultural leadership of the West," finds an unabashed confidence and exhilaration in the promise of America: "At home and abroad in the 1920s, the nation was usually referred to not as the 'United States' but as 'America.' ... Americans in the 1920s liked the term 'America' precisely for its imperial suggestions of an intoxicating and irresistible identity windswept into coherence by the momentum of destiny; this generation had little reason to anticipate history's hardest lessons."[8]

What led people in the 1920s to embrace the term "America" leads many people in the United States and throughout the world today to reject it. These "imperial suggestions of an intoxicating and irresistible identity" led us to take as ours alone the name of a whole continent, thus denying in language what we nullified in foreign policies —the equal integrity and importance of Canada, the equal integrity and independence of Mexico and Latin America. I recognize the limits of the term and yet use it intentionally and ironically. We are once again engaged in a process of national identity formation. Conservatives are right: the myth of America, or the vision of American innocence, beneficence, and global pre-eminence, is no longer secure. What does it mean to speak of America after the lessons of history— the lessons of McCarthyism, the internment of Japanese Americans, American military interventions in Latin America, Vietnam, and Watergate, and the persistence of racism and sexism? Recall the words of Malcolm X: "The American dream looks like a nightmare to me."[9] Many see the America dream as a nightmare at worst, a delusion at best: the reality of downsizing and job loss; massive cuts in social services; the mandate for people on welfare to get jobs in the absence of an economy that provides affordable, high quality child care, or jobs at a living wage; violence, hopelessness, homelessness, and anger: the anger of white males at women and minorities for supposedly getting "their jobs," the anger and violence of a marginalized urban underclass, the fear and desperation of women trapped in abusive relationships and low-paying jobs.[10]

How do we address those fears?

There are many solutions to America's ills. Some are protectionist and nostalgic, if not downright reactionary, calls for a return to an imagined America of strong families and cohesive communities, an

America of traditional values, of traditional roles for women and men, calls for an end to the "culture of complaint," with women and racial minorities content to work hard and accept as equitable the current social contract and distribution of educational and economic opportunity. Some advocate a return to the imagined America of our childhoods, one of global pre-eminence, somehow attained and maintained without coercion or violence; an America without doubts, an America that can overcome all limits.

And where are democrats, progressives, and leftists in this collective malaise? Where are we in these debates over women's rights as human rights, in debates over economic justice? We are floundering in a sea of humane and compassionate aspirations and mind-boggling limits to fulfilling even basic human needs, struggling with the limits of state and federal resources to fund education, health care, reproductive choice, infrastructure maintenance, and basic city services.

What does it mean to be American at this time of fundamental economic restructuring, of mutually exclusive definitions of fundamental human rights, of intractable forms of international tension, of ongoing challenges of race and sex discrimination, of violence and gross disparities in economic opportunity? What do the challenges and tensions of postcolonialism mean for the colonizers? Can we shift from a culture of conquest—masked, of course, as a culture of benign and beneficent progress, expansion, and vitality—to an equally vital culture of living with limits, with ambiguity, and with a self-critical recognition of our own abuses of power? Yes, if we realize that ambiguity and self-critique do not necessarily lead to humility or resignation, but can be a concomitant of audacious creativity and exuberant and fluid group identity. Such a shift is possible and marks as significant a challenge to the logic of social protest as it does to the logic of national identity and pride.

I offer another myth of America, a myth that combines vitality with the recognition of Malcolm X's American nightmare and the bedrock perdurability of limits. I still use the term "America" to refer to our national identity at this time turning, of possibility, of learning to keep the vitality and energy of the American dream of prosperity, of democracy, of freedom, along with a recognition of failure, excesses, unintended consequences, and limits.

Old dreams of progress, of freedom, of unbridled and unlimited economic growth no longer resonate, no longer inspire and motivate. What is left? Apathy, despair, cynicism, a focus on merely individual well-being? No. It is possible to create and resist without the illusion of progress. It is possible to live fully and well without hopes for ultimate victory and certain vindication. In this book I celebrate the energy and joy of politics without utopia, ethics without virtue, and spirituality without God.

Stage 5. How do we understand the chaos and complexity of social change? How do we understand our identities as actors in social systems, when we realize that the very structures of agency, of knowledge, and of imagination are shaped by complex and contradictory forms of discourse?

In order to describe a form of power and a means of colonizing desire (Foucault) that can energize the self-critical and creative formation of institutions and community structures, I explore the contradictions and complexities of what I am presenting as a postmodern humanism. Just the phrase, postmodern humanism, is of course a contradiction in terms. Central to postmodern philosophy is a critique of any attempts to ground epistemology or political claims in any discernible or given essence of "human being."

I will argue nonetheless for a critical humanism, for a turn to humanism as the site of engaging different claims about not only social policy but also the very nature of good and evil, of justice, order, power, and chaos. Feminists, men and women involved in the Religious Right, in communitarianism, in the politics of meaning, all are engaged in the construction of group and individual identity, in often mutually exclusive constructions of what it means to be human. To turn to humanism, then, is not to find an answer, an ahistorical or essential resolution to this debate, but rather to name what is at stake—radically different constructions of order, radically different ways of engaging chaos, radically different views of what sustains creativity and community, of that which prevents injustice and cruelty.

I argue, then, for humanism as the site of cultural and political debate, and argue as well for a specific construction of humanity.

In contrast to the humanism of Emerson and Feuerbach, a humanism that exalts our capacity for reason or transcendence, I propose a nondualistic understanding of human being, both individually and collectively, that takes as constitutive our capacity for courage and error, for insight and illusion, for compassion, self-deception, and harm. Taking the model of conjure as developed by Theophus Smith, I argue that ethical power consists not in ridding ourselves of this proclivity for harm, illusion, and error, but rather in the creative working within the matrix of human lives that are always conditioned historically, and subject to fault and short-sightedness.[11]

What do we do when we question the myth of the fundamental corruptibility of the oppressor and the inevitably reliable and resilient wisdom of the oppressed? How do we exercise power, knowing that both groups are capable of insight and self-serving delusion? How do we act, think, and judge when the old script of Revolution no longer makes sense? How do we continue to take seriously poverty, hunger, and war when denunciation of those evils in itself no longer offers any comfort? The evils are identified, those responsible and complicit castigated, and then what? Who provides effective antiracist training for police departments? Who enables companies to be accountable to locales, both human and natural? How do we prevent famine? What are the concomitants of a just and durable peace agreement between Israelis and Palestinians? How do we provide jobs, hope, and a place to thrive for an estranged, desperately poor underclass?

Part of this essay is grounded in the simple matter of growing up and realizing that there is no one else to complain *to*, to denounce or challenge, no other adults who will hear our cries of injustice and transform reality. The myth—"denounce the evil and those in power will redress it," is inadequate. We *are* the ones in charge, in small ways and in large. We are the voters, the parents, the teachers, the owners and managers of business, the investors, the government officials. What do *we* do when the protest is heard? The old myth—"Give power to those marginalized and we will transform the world"—no longer comforts. Once we have power, and we should have it, what are we to do with it? How do we move from the politics of protest to the very different challenges of building institutions?

This essay is written, therefore, for those disillusioned with socialist rallying cries. It's for those for whom "Workers of the world unite!" has a rather hollow ring. What do we do *when* we unite? Unions can become corrupt; socialist governments can become oppressive and unjust. How do we live without the myth that we are more pure than our "capitalist oppressors?" I would not say that we are any worse, but I do not think that we are any wiser, any kinder, any less subject to pettiness and to the abuse of power. Gaining power, gaining a voice, is only a fragment of the challenge. Granted, it is an essential ingredient, but we do not necessarily know how to set up a fair health care system, how to reform the judiciary, how to change the penal system or international monetary systems. Too many leftist critiques assume such answers will emerge readily once power is in the hands of the "right" people. They don't.

This essay emerges, therefore, from attention to the pettiness of even the oppressed, to the limits of strategy and vision of the marginalized as well as the limits of knowledge and insight of those with relatively more power.

This book is an examination of what it means to live out Kantian ethical expectations in a world of continental limits. That is, we are still shaped by expectations of the categorical imperative ("Act only on that maxim through which you can at the same time will that it should become a universal law")[12] and yet our very ability to act, the extent to which we are in any sense individuals, is itself historically and culturally constructed, malleable, and contested. We are not autonomous agents, attempting to exercise revealed or discerned ideals, but the creatures of social and political forces that exist outside us. Although continental philosophy has helped us articulate the ways in which our subjectivity is constructed and constituted, I build on this work to examine what it means to act ethically, acknowledging that the self who acts is a creative fiction, and that this same socially constituted self is also the matrix in which we live.

Stage 6. Finally, I will address explicitly the nature of spirituality, and argue for an integration of spirituality and political work. I will describe a nontheistic yet ecstatic and mystical humanism. This type of spirituality is also intrinsically paradoxical. Ecstatic religious experience, the phenomenon of group cohesion, of being buoyed and supported by others, by forces larger than oneself, is both an essential component of sustained work for justice and fundamentally amoral. That is, the experience of transcendence is not foundational. It is an experience of creativity, connection, and energy that is as likely to be evoked by the Religious Right and by the Klan, as by politically progressive religious groups. The sense of religious ecstasy in each is the same: the sense of being energized, of being connected with forces outside oneself. The fact that a group feels a tremendous surge of vitality says nothing about either the truth of its claims about reality or the legitimacy of its projects for cultural and community formation. Our criteria, our means of adjudicating these claims, remain as contested and open as ever. I argue that we need a critical humanism to check our claims about deity, about the good, and that the check to fanaticism is not religious but political, a critical examination of the actual impact on people of a community's constructions of good, order, truth, and power.

I will return here to Theophus Smith's understanding of conjure: that which heals, also harms. The notion of effective spiritual and political power cannot be captured in the confines of binary logic; spiritual power, ethical power, even our work for justice—none of these markers of a meaningful and profound life is wholly good or wholly evil. The strengths that people bring to political work, to institutions, are inextricably tied to our weaknesses. Rather than seeking to excise these weaknesses in either the interests of efficiency or spiritual purity, I depict an alternative logic of ethical and spiritual power: practices, concepts, and images that acknowledge the ambiguity of power, a logic that enables a community to work for justice without self-righteousness, without humility, without fanaticism, and without naiveté about the likely abuses of power.

I see the book itself as a work of conjure, an example of the rhetoric of invitation. I offer here not specific proposals for economic transformation and political change but a lens for seeing the contours of the multifaceted political, economic, and cultural challenges that face us. I offer here not a resolution of our manifold political crises but a moral vocabulary, a grammar for naming the options we construct. I offer here not answers but ways of acting without closure, without definitive analyses, and without guarantees.

I

Virtuosity

Jazz was a struggle which pitted mind against the perversity of circumstance, and . . . in this struggle blinding virtuosity was the best weapon.
　　—Eric Lott, "Double V, Double-Time: Bebop's Politics of Style"

Given the persistence of injustice, given the ongoing challenges of social inequality, many people question our comforting myths of cultural progress, political reform, and institutional change. In the United States, while the right wing continues to espouse a moral and political vocabulary of progress, truth, and moral certainty, to many of us who are liberal and progressive, that same vocabulary seems increasingly untenable. The dynamics of political change are hardly clear-cut—an easy move from identifying forms of injustice, mobilizing people to challenge the institutional bulwarks of injustice, dismantling those institutional structures, and then replacing them with just structures managed by fair-minded people committed to equality, justice, and freedom. The journey to fundamental political change is far more circuitous.

In *The Alchemy of Race and Rights*, for example, Patricia Williams explores the failures and successes of rights discourse in the United States. She depicts a phenomenon that is far from the simple application of absolute truths to changing situations, far from a steady progression of expanding rights. She describes, rather, a complex process in which imperfectly articulated and framed rights are applied sporadically and unevenly to alleviate and/or challenge misery and injustice.[1]

In Derrick Bell's *And We Are Not Yet Saved: The Elusive Quest for Racial Justice*, we find a sobering analysis of the ways in which "society implemented its commitment to ending racial segregation—only to replace it with more effective, if less obvious, forms of white dominance. The new techniques, unlike the vanquished Jim Crow practices, were immune to legal attack."[2] In his second book, *Faces at the Bottom of the Well: The Permanence of Racism*, Bell analyzes the drastically reduced economic opportunities for working-class blacks, the diminishing opportunities for the "most fortunate" blacks, and argues that these economic developments are grounded in "a social structure where the subordination of blacks serves many whites as a basis of personal identity and social stability."[3] To call this racism permanent does not mean giving up the struggle for racial justice, but manifests a "tardy recognition of racism's deepest roots."[4] In his third book, *Gospel Choirs: Psalms of Survival in an Alien Land Called Home*, Bell takes up the challenge of describing cultural resources that can elicit new forms of collective activism in response to ongoing sexism and racial hostility.

The uneven march to racial justice is not unique. In work for equality between women and men, in trying to create a world without the threat of nuclear war, there are gains and losses: achievements followed by new challenges and threats. The end of the Cold War has brought a significant reduction in the threat of a globally disastrous nuclear war, yet we now face the challenges of ethnic tensions (Bosnia, for example) and the political and economic restructuring of the former Soviet Union and the Eastern bloc.

How do we respond to the persistence of injustice? Garth Kasimu Baker-Fletcher, writing of "the mood, the sense, and the feeling of being a Black man in an environment dominated by values, mores, and customs inimical to healthy self-affirmation of Blackness," speaks of the need to hold together "disappointment, frustration, rage, disenchantment, disillusionment, and determination," and coins a new word—disillragedeterminassion.[5] I share Baker-Fletcher's search for categories that combine the seemingly incompatible, the mutually exclusive yet simultaneously present longings for justice, rage at suffering, and forthright recognition of our own shortsightedness, complicity, and limits. Unlike Kasimu Baker-Fletcher, however, I coin no words but instead turn to jazz, to chaos theory, to the history of social justice movements, to the joys and challenges of teaching to find vision, hope, commitment, and responsibility without the illusion of progress or certain victory.

Taking seriously our defeats, the defeats and inadequacies of even the revolutionary vanguard, can lead to cynicism and/or to individual withdrawal. In one of her poems, "Those Who Come After," Eleanor Wilner captures well a mood of waiting, of honesty, of openness in the face of the demise of old myths.

> Those Who Come After
> will never say of us:
> *What wonderful myths they had.*
> ... what we leave
> is all that can be
> dredged up from wrecked harbors—
> history's debris.[6]

We face the loss of "wonderful myths," of "being more than ourselves," and in not hiding from that loss, something does emerge. Wilner's image of that emergence is wistful and slight:

> But when they say of us
> what we have done, perhaps they will speak
> kindly of those who, near the century's
> end, pried open the hand;
> ... perhaps they will
> say that there were those
> who took down the harps
> hung in the sorrowing trees, having lost
> the taste for conquest or revenge,
> and made a song
> that rose in the air
> as smoke rises—[7]

This essay is such a song—metaphors of energy, vitality, and power to replace the certitudes of Us Against Them on the Road to Certain Victory.

Where can we find such a mythos, a narrative to guide us in finding beauty in ambiguity, failure, resilience, and inconclusivity? So many of our western myths, our narratives of progress, of freedom, democracy, and prosperity, seem to be predicated on the disavowal of ambiguity and limits. Heroes transcend their flaws in the rousing pursuit of grand ends—their goals being universal peace, the war to end all wars, liberty and justice for all.

Charles Krauthammer describes the "unheroic nature of our times," and contrasts it with the sensibility expressed by John F. Kennedy in his inaugural address:

> For an idea of what a heroic time sounds like, read the Inaugural Address of John Kennedy. By sentence 4, Kennedy had outlined the stakes, the drama of his era. Today, he declared, "man holds in his mortal hands the power to abolish all forms of human poverty and all forms of human life." The eradication of poverty. Salvation from Armageddon. These are biblical tasks. Kennedy took them as his own.[8]

Where do we go when the myths of heroes and grand causes no longer incite us or evoke passion and energy? Where do we go when revolutions fail? How do we act without the comforting mooring of thinking that ours is the defining moment, not just in human history but also in the very evolution of life; that ours is the pinnacle in the drama of life on earth, the culmination of the evolution of physical complexity, heightened sensory and conceptual awareness, and the achievement of an intricate, creative, and productive civilization?

In *Wonderful Life*, Stephen Jay Gould argues that the model of evolutionary progress that we have been taught from childhood—the comforting story of evolutionary development from single-celled organisms to human life in all its individual and social complexity, is, quite simply, wrong. The idea that life has progressed, moving from a few simple life forms to many complex ones, is not borne out by the fossil record. He describes the startling discovery and interpretation of the Burgess Shale and its implications for our understanding of evolution and of ourselves. Rather than a few simple precursors of later more complex forms of life, the Burgess Shale contains a disparity in anatomical plans far greater than exists today. Dating from the "Cambrian explosion" 570 million years ago, "the creatures from this single quarry in British Columbia probably exceed, in anatomical range, the entire spectrum of invertebrate life in today's oceans."[9] Not only was there initially great disparity, but there also appears to be no obvious reason for the decimation of the many and the survival of the few. Darwinian notions of the survival of the fittest cannot be applied to the Burgess Shale with any confidence.

> Groups may prevail or die for reasons that bear no relationship to the Darwinian basis of success in normal times. Even if fishes hone their adaptations to peaks of aquatic perfection, they will all die if the ponds dry up. But grubby old Buster the Lungfish, former laughingstock of the piscine priesthood, may pull through—and not because a bunion on his great-grandfather's fin warned his ancestors about an impending comet. Buster and his kin may prevail because a feature evolved long ago for a different use has fortuitously permitted survival during a sudden and unpredictable change in rules. And if we are Buster's legacy, and the result of a thousand other similarly happy accidents, how can we possibly view our mentality as inevitable, or even probable?[10]

Gould claims that these discoveries have wide ethical import—leading him to question how we account for our place in the scheme of life, how we assess the meaning of the human enterprise.

> If humanity arose just yesterday as a small twig on one branch of a flourishing tree, then life may not, in any genuine sense, exist for us or because of us. Perhaps we are only an afterthought, a kind of cosmic accident, just one bauble on the Christmas tree of evolution.
>
> What options are left in the face of geology's most frightening fact? ... We may, as this book advocates, accept the implications

and learn to seek the meaning of human life, including the source of morality, in other, more appropriate, domains—either stoically with a sense of loss, or with joy in the challenge if our temperament be optimistic.[11]

Just as Gould questions the familiar story of linear evolution, a complex process destined to produce us, so many activists are questioning the comforting myths of cultural progress, political reform, and institutional change. What happens when we take seriously the open-ended nature of our work for social justice? Our actions often have unintended consequences. It may be "Buster the Lungfish": the debates that occur because of our mistakes (e.g., replicating homophobic stereotypes as we attempt to challenge homophobia) that moves a group forward. How do we live with the surprises, contradictions, and failures that attend social action?

There is a way to live with ambiguity and to evoke power, group identity, and vitality without scapegoating and self-righteousness. I see this sensibility in Gould, in Andrew Hayes's application of chaos theory to legal reasoning, in Molly Ivins's political commentaries, and in jazz.

In his explication of the essentials of chaos theory and the metaphors for social and political power that it implies, Andrew Hayes claims that the focus of chaos theory is complexity and irregularity in nature and society.

> Where chaos begins, classical science stops. For as long as the world has had physicists inquiring into the laws of nature, it has suffered a special ignorance about disorder in the atmosphere, in the turbulent sea, in the fluctuations of wild life populations, in the iterations of the heart and the brain. The irregular side of nature, the discontinuous and erratic side—these have been puzzles to science, or worse, monstrosities.[12]

By paying attention to turbulence and flux, researchers claim to have found a "new kind of order—a structured disorder in which simple deterministic equations generate endlessly complex, infinitely detailed, yet non-random results."[13]

What does this mean for evolution and progress? Gould's theory of evolution, based on the Burgess Shale, is one of chaotic evolution.

> Gould replaced Darwin's deterministic axiom of survival of the fittest and his implicit teleological assumption that species are constantly evolving towards some higher state of being with a theory of chaotic evolution in which chance and randomness play an essential role, progress is stochastic rather than linear, and progress itself means only endless adaptation without any fixed goal.[14]

Hayes finds in chaos theory a model for authority and legitimacy within the practice and theory of law. Acknowledging that legal reasoning is constituted by the interplay of "principle and counterprinciple, general rule and exception," Hayes questions the false dichotomy between legal reasoning as the application of established principles or as a nihilistic political struggle:

> This new idea of the space in which legal reasoning takes place calls into question the critiques of manipulability and indeterminacy, according to which the existing system of rules is a facade because any given rule is either indeterminate or has a counter-rule that can be invoked at the desired occasion without any principled distinction between the two. This implicitly assumes that legal reasoning exists in a Cartesian world in which principles are straight lines with clear boundaries, and the only alternative is to confess that law is just a mask for free-form political struggle.[15]

The alternative is a form of reasoning as applicable to social critique and policy formation as it is to legal reasoning:

> Like a fractal object that reveals new levels of complexity as it is examined at greater and greater levels of detail, legal doctrine has an infinite capacity to elaborate itself in response to new factual contexts, raising new questions for each answer. And maddeningly (for some), this process is nondeterministic: law is forever making progress, but never quite arrives.[16]

Hayes concludes his article by evoking the beauty and joy of working within the horizon of nonlinear, changing, but never finalized complexity.

It is here that we can see the beginnings of a "cultural metaphor" of energy, vitality, and power to replace the certitudes of Us Against Them on the Road to Certain Victory. Hayes describes the beauty of the dynamic process of legal reasoning. Political columnist Molly Ivins depicts, in her commentaries, another essential dimension of power without self-righteousness, a recognition of the absurdities of the chaotic, nonlinear, surprising twists and turns of political life:

> Fellow citizens, as we stagger toward the millennium, I can only hope that this modest oeuvre—as we often say in Amarillo—will remind you that we need to stop and laugh along the way. We live in a Great Nation, but those who attempt to struggle through it unarmed with a sense of humor are apt to wind up in my Aunt Eula's Fort Worth Home for the Terminally Literal-Minded, gibbering like some demented neoconservative about the Decline of Civilization.
>
> Any nation that can survive what we have lately in the way of government is on the high road to permanent glory. So hang in there, keep fightin' for freedom, raise more hell, and don't forget to laugh, too.
>
> Yours in the belief that the Founders were right all along, but that the results are a lot funnier than they intended.[17]

We can learn a simple, surprisingly liberating lesson from Gould, Hayes, and Ivins: stop fighting chaos—accept it, roll with it, relish the challenge it offers, and be unabashedly amazed at the results. The results of our attempts to teach well, of our efforts at social change, are sometimes as peculiar in their own right as any of the organisms found in the Burgess Shale (I find, for example, that many committees are remarkably akin to Hallucigenia, a creature supported by seven pairs of struts and having no readily discernible mechanisms for either eating or moving).[18]

Once again, Gould expresses the challenge succinctly and vividly:

> Homo sapiens, I fear, is a "thing so small" in a vast universe, a wildly improbable evolutionary event well within the realm of

contingency. Make of such a conclusion what you will. Some
find the prospect depressing; I have always regarded it as exhilarating, and a source of both freedom and consequent moral
responsibility.[19]

What a ride this life is!—not easy, often tragic, but one that, even
without the solace of clear answers, evokes all of our power—the
power of our intellects, our imaginations, our hearts. Now who would
expect that any collection of fallible, eccentric, imperfect human
beings, putting all of our energy into living well and living fully would
produce anything but surprise after surprise?

It may be well and good to acknowlege the likelihood of the
unlikely, the predictability of the unpredictable, but how do we live
with surprise? While novelty may be welcome as part of entertainment, how do we incorporate unpredictability into our very concepts
of group and national identity? Can we have identity as a nation without definitions, without clear parameters, without necessary and lasting characteristics? What would the honest acceptance of limits and
unpredictability mean for our understanding of America and the
American dream?

Before we embrace too readily the surprises of chaos theory and
celebrate too wholeheartedly the exhilaration of indeterminacy and
creativity, it is important that we remember the costs of such complexity and ambiguity in human lives. As Derrick Bell and Patricia
Williams teach us in their analyses of the checkered struggle for racial
justice, not all surprises are benign or exhilarating.

It is here that postmodern analyses of political power and social
movements are most helpful. In the work of Foucault, for example, we
find not just an analysis of the partiality and fallibility of particular systems of order, truth, and goodness, but also a recognition of the function of failure, contradiction, exclusion, and limitation in those
systems. In his study of madness and psychiatry, crime and punishment, illness and clinical medicine, Foucault "tried to show how we
have indirectly constituted ourselves through the exclusion of some
other: criminals, mad people and so on."[20] In *Discipline and Punish,* he
demonstrates that

> Efforts to institute "less cruelty, less suffering, more gentleness, more respect, more 'humanity'," have had the perverse effect of reinventing the entirety of modern society on the model of a prison, imposing ever more subtle, and insidiously punishing kinds of "discipline," not just on convicts, but also on soldiers, on workers, on students, even on the various professionals trained to supervise various "disciplinary" institutions, in the process refining new "corrective technologies of the individual"—and producing a "double effect: a 'soul' to be known and a subjection to be maintained."[21]

In his genealogies Foucault provides detailed accounts of the ways in which the ideals of reason and of humanism can be used to support domination and injustice.[22] He poses a sharp question to modernist and postmodern thinkers:

> How can we exist as rational beings, fortunately committed to practicing a rationality that is unfortunately crisscrossed by intrinsic dangers? ... One should not forget ... it was on the basis of the flamboyant rationality of social Darwinism that racism was formulated, becoming one of the most enduring and powerful ingredients of Nazism.[23]

Given the ambiguity of reason, what is the role of criticism? "It is precisely to accept this sort of spiral, this sort of revolving door of rationality that refers us to its necessity, to its indispensability, and at the same time, to its intrinsic dangers."[24]

Foucault's critique is far-reaching. He does not stop with denouncing the new forms of coercive power exercised by liberal reformers. He has also challenged the Left to recognize the disparity between ideals and practices in our movements for social change, and challenged us to examine the function of those disparities in intent and effect.[25]

It is this aspect of Foucault's work that James Miller claims is a challenge to "American Foucauldians."

> Most of these latter-day American Foucauldians are high-minded democrats; they are committed to forging a more diverse society in which whites and people of color, straights and gays, men and women, their various ethnic and gender "differences"

intact, can nevertheless all live together in compassionate harmony—an appealing if difficult goal, with deep roots in the
Judeo-Christian tradition. Unfortunately, Foucault's lifework,
as I have come to understand it, is far more unconventional—
and far more discomfiting—than some of his "progressive"
admirers seem ready to admit. Unless I am badly mistaken,
Foucault issued a brave and basic challenge to nearly everything
that passes for "right" in Western culture—including nearly
everything that passes for "right" among a great many of
America's left-wing academics.[26]

How do we think, judge, and act if we accept Foucault's critique of
Enlightenment humanism and liberal and leftist politics—at the core
of rationality, irrationality, at the core of humanism, domination and
exclusion? What were the political strategies practiced by Foucault,
and what are alternative political responses to his analysis of the politics of truth?[27]

The trajectory of Foucault's attempts to foster political activism
outside the founding categories of humanism and universal moral
truth is clear. He moved from a glorification of transgression, destruction, and violent political revolution to a commitment to unrelenting
social critique and, later, to an emphasis on the technology of the self.

Foucault's early work is marked by an ambiguous and evocative
analysis of transgression and violence.[28] From his critique of humanism and his study of madness and civilization, Foucault came to reject
the central goal of humanism, the production of happiness:

> I believe that humanism, at least on the level of politics, might be
> defined as every attitude that considers the aim of politics to be
> the production of happiness. Now, I do not think that the notion
> of happiness is truly thinkable. Happiness does not exist—and
> the happiness of men still less.[29]

Miller correctly demonstrates that Foucault's alternative to happiness was the "shared rapture" of "untamed collective energy."[30] He
states that as early as 1953, Foucault had declared that "man can and
must experience himself negatively, through hate and aggression."[31]

Foucault moved from a fascination with individual madness and cruelty to a celebration of political violence.[32]

> Emboldened by his own "limit-experience" of politics fifteen years later, first in Tunisia, then in France, he had participated in pitched battles with the police; he had helped foment discontent in French prisons; and, contemplating with evident equanimity the bloodshed in popular revolts, he had called for destroying "the unity of society."[33]

Miller provides a description of revolt endorsed by Foucault, the "intoxicating disorder" of the Parisian student revolts of May 1968.

> Billboards were ripped apart, sign posts uprooted, scaffolding and barbed wire pulled down, parked cars tipped over. Piles of debris mounted in the middle of the boulevards. The mood was giddy, the atmosphere festive. "Everyone instantly recognized the reality of their desires," one participant wrote shortly afterward, summing up the prevailing spirit, "never had the passion for destruction been shown to be more creative." ... That Monday, more than one million people filled the streets of Paris. The student revolt had turned into a general protest against the authoritarianism of the Gaullist state—and, less clearly but more explosively, against the very order of things in the modern world generally.[34]

The basis of this creativity was the power of transgression, overturning the hypocrisies of moralism and humanism, a creativity reduced, in May 1968, to a slogan: "Soyons Cruels!"[35] What did it mean for Foucault to advocate cruelty? Miller's list of the possibilities suggested by Foucault is stark, taking transgression as the fundamental marker of individual and societal creativity:

> —BE CRUEL in your quest for the truth, ruthless in your honesty, savage in your irreverence ...
> —BE CRUEL in your resoluteness, welcome the harsh renunciations and sometimes brutal costs of relentlessly pursuing any vaulting ideal, be it truth, godliness, or revolutionary purity ...
> —BE CRUEL in the works of imagination that you create: spare nothing in painting the demons in the desert who tempt

Saint Anthony:...give us the death of Damiens in unbearable
detail...
—BE CRUEL in your erotic play: ... savor the disintegra-
tion and humiliation of the self in the *jouissance* of exploded limits...
—BE CRUEL in the license you give to individual acts and
political practices that issue in suffering and death: sing the
praises of murderers, unrestrained sovereigns, and bloody
movements of popular revolt...[36]

The wager here is clear: "better externalized than internalized cruelty."[37]

This stage of Foucault's political work was sharply modified after
1975. Foucault recognized that it was this very logic that unleashed the
horrors of Fascism and the Holocaust. In the Holocaust, "Be Cruel"
was "accomplished as history."[38]

If the task of the revolutionary is no longer the destruction of social
order, unleashing the "unbound powers" of chaos and "instinctive violence," what is the fitting response to social injustice and the abuse of
power?[39] In his work with prisoners, and in his study of the function
of the prison in modern society, *Discipline and Punish*, Foucault
describes the task of the intellectual as unrelenting social critique.

It is not up to us to suggest a reform ... We wish only to make
known the reality. And to make it known instantly, nearly day
by day: for the issue is pressing. We must alert opinion, and keep
it alert.[40]

Foucault's stance is like that advocated by some Quakers and many
leftists in the United States. The challenge of those who are oppressed
and marginalized is simple, unrelenting, and clear: Speak Truth to
Power.

In response to those immobilized by his description of the normalizing and repressive effects of supposedly humanistic penal reforms,
Foucault claimed that such paralysis was precisely the point. He wanted to break down the simple division between good and evil, the
"social and moral distinctions between the innocent and the guilty."[41]

> It's true that certain people, such as those who work in the insti-
> tutional setting of the prison ... are not likely to find advice or
> instruction in my books to tell them "what is to be done." But
> my project is precisely to bring it about that they "no longer
> know what to do," so that the acts, gestures, discourses that up
> until then had seemed to go without saying become problematic,
> difficult, dangerous.[42]

In his last work, Foucault took up another challenge. Although he
did not propose specific political actions, he did examine the "technology of the self" from ancient Greece through the modern period,
attempting to replace the "fascist in us all" through changing consciousness and transforming institutions.

> How ... does one keep from being fascist, even (especially)
> when one believes oneself to be a revolutionary militant? How
> do we rid our speech and our acts, our hearts and our pleasures
> of fascism? How do we ferret out the fascism that is ingrained in
> our behavior?[43]

This concern led Foucault to advocate and practice a conjunction
of individual and social change:

> I would rather oppose actual experiences than the possiblility of
> a utopia. It is possible that the rough outlines of a future society
> is supplied by the recent experiences with drugs, sex, communes,
> other forms of consciousness, and other forms of individuality. If
> scientific socialism emerged from the *Utopias* of the nineteenth
> century, it is possible that a real socialization will emerge, in the
> twentieth century, from *experiences*.[44]

Foucault tried to find a new vocabulary for power, tried to escape
the logic of transgression, and yet his intimations of such a possible
world remain slight, the attraction of violence and suffering profound.
Foucault endorsed the "rapture" of the Iranian revolution despite its
horrific violence.[45] His radical politics of the self was expressed through
the "suffering-pleasure" he experienced in the sado-masochistic sexual practices of part of the gay community in France and the United
States.[46]

Despite his evocation of "suffering-pleasure," Foucault tried to envision the possibility of limits without repression, of creativity without cruelty. Yet, this possibility, a "technology of the self" beyond the love of violence and "self-chosen torture," eluded him:

> Have we found a positive foundation, instead of self-sacrifice, for the hermeneutics of the self? I cannot say this, no. We have tried, at least from the humanistic period of the Renaissance till now. *And we can't find it.*"[47]

Foucault could not find a technology of the self founded on life, rather than death, on the affirmation, rather than the negation of the self.

What was not possible for Foucault *is* possible for us. We exist at a different juncture in history. Twenty years after Foucault's critique of revolutionary violence and the "fascist in us all" it is possible to see *and feel* the limits of the "shared rapture" of destruction. The glorification of destructive power has lost its allure. The focus on transgression as an end in itself is as much a failure of the intellect and imagination as it is of the heart. Revolutionary violence is horrific in its waste of lives, absurd in its equation of destruction with creativity. Not only are we fully aware of the human costs of the Iranian revolution, we know the ravages of violence and terror in Rwanda, the tragedy of "ethnic cleansing" in Bosnia.

The excess of transgression is deadly; the excess of transgression is also intellectually vapid. Miller provides a telling comment, the later reflections of one who participated in the May 1968 revolt:

> "The fact was that to anyone who asked rationally enough 'What do you want?' I had no answer," a professed Maoist recalled years later. "I couldn't say that I didn't even know who these comrades were, couldn't say that I was demonstrating for the sake of demonstrating."[48]

If we are no longer thrilled by the prospect of "demonstrating for the sake of demonstrating," what are our options? The prospect of unrelenting social critique is similarly a failure of intellect, of creativity, and of solidarity. To take as one's role merely the challenge of critique, merely the goal of Speaking Truth to Power, is to delude ourselves in regard to our own power, our own lack of innocence, and our own capacities for institutional and system-building creativity. What is the alternative? *Use power truthfully.* Even the revolts, marches, boycotts, sit-ins, and demonstrations of those outside economic and political institutions are an expression of power, not powerlessness. We can acknowledge the power of these techniques and be aware of the ways in which we are as likely to abuse power as those we denounce, likely to abuse power within our organizations for social change, likely to abuse power in the partiality of our efforts for social transformation.

To *use power truthfully* moves us to the challenge of responding to protest, implementing reform, acting in full awareness of the danger and unpredictability of our interventions.

How, then, do we act? Here is our dilemma: In the analysis of political problems, even when we are right, we may lose. As for our political strategies, what worked once, or in one place, may not work again; our coalitions are essential and intrinsically fragile (people working for the same goals, but with different reasons, or sharing the same values but advocating mutually exclusive strategies); and the participants in all of our work for justice—us, the leaders, and the workers—are flawed and imperfect, for once we get power we are as likely to abuse it as anyone else.

The result of such awareness does not have to be violence, cynicism, or resignation. There are cultural metaphors of energy and vitality that can come from working with obstacles, limits, ambiguity, and transience. There is a positive foundation for the hermeneutics of the self. The model that I present comes from jazz.[49]

Why jazz? Because, to quote Jed Rasula, I have "learned from jazz how to hear the world differently."[50] I have learned from jazz how to work with limits and opportunities, possibility and ambiguity, obstacles and challenges. I see in jazz a model of meaning, a model of responsiveness without progress or repetition, without self-abnegation or self-righteousness.

Many theorists and novelists claim that jazz offers a profound metaphor for the dynamics of community building and social responsibility. Toni Cade Bambara explores the dynamics of social responsibility in her novel *The Salteaters*.[51] She uses jazz to explain what it means to work for social justice when you do not know which issue to respond to first (racism, sexism, economic exploitation, or environmental degradation), and, in the response, when you find your own allies fighting you and each other over the best strategy. Should the focus be primarily political or spiritual? If the focus is political, which politics, and if the focus is spiritual, which religious traditions? Bambara asks, how do we go on acting when we do not have the answers, when we know that we ourselves, far from being the prophetic vanguard, are often as much a part of the problem as part of the solution? Bambara describes an activist who sees this dilemma and then discovers that the answer is there in her own community. She claims that the creative energy of jazz is a model for the creative energy of politics.

> She could dance right off the stool, her head thrown back and singing, cheering, celebrating all those giants she had worshipped in their terrible musicalness. Giant teachers teaching through tone and courage and inventiveness but scorned, rebuked, beleaguered, trivialized, commercialized, copied, plundered, goofed on by half-upright pianos and droopy-drawers drums and horns too long in hock and spittin' up rust and blood, tormented by sleazy bookers and takers, tone-deaf amateurs and saboteurs, … underpaid and overworked till they didn't know, didn't trust, wouldn't move on the wonderful gift given and were mute, crazy and beat-up. But standing up in their genius anyway ready to speak the unpronounceable. On the stand with no luggage and no maps and ready to go anywhere in the universe together on just sheer holy boldness.[52]

Jazz is part of the cultural resources of Americans. I think that it functions—as art often does—to lead the way, to configure insights and sensibilities only later brought to conceptual expression. Theophus Smith, for example, sees gospel, jazz, and the blues as an integral part of social transformation, what he calls "conjure." Smith analyzes the power of blues songs "to transcend negative experiences and feelings by recapitulating or reprising the negative, but precisely in such a way (ecstatically) that they transform the negative."[53] How does this happen? Despair, anger, and grief are expressed, but the expression is itself vital, ironic, and compelling, the very articulation of limits and loss, an escape from being defined solely by loss, solely by limits, solely by rage and despair. Smith cites James Baldwin's account of the irony and transcendence expressed in blues, gospel and jazz. He hears in "some gospel songs, for example, and in jazz, . . . and especially in the blues . . . something tart and ironic, authoritative and double-edged. (By contrast) white Americans seem to feel that happy songs are happy and sad songs are sad."[54]

Gerald Early also speaks of the power of jazz. He claims that "R & B and jazz were of a piece, part of a grand continuum in black life."[55] He states that "jazz tell[s] the same story as R&B . . . the tale of how black folk soar above adversity. I realized that black music was the most telling criticism of American life."[56]

Even though gospel, blues, and jazz express a "telling criticism of American life," they also express an affirmation of life, a way of creating and living in the face of ambiguity and limits. Ralph Ellison highlights this dimension of jazz:

> Now, I had learned from the jazz musicians I had known as a boy in Oklahoma City something of the discipline and devotion to his art required of the artists. . . . These jazzmen, many of them now world-famous, lived for and with music intensely. Their driving motivation was neither money nor fame, but the will to achieve the most eloquent expression of idea-emotions through the technical mastery of their instruments . . . and the give and take, the subtle rhythmical shaping and blending of idea, tone and imagination demanded of group improvisation. The delicate balance struck between strong individual personality and the group during those early jam sessions was a marvel of social organization. I had learned too that the end of all this discipline and technical mastery was the desire to express an affirmative way of life through its musical tradition and that this tradition insisted that each artist achieve his creativity within its frame. He must learn the best of the past, and add to it his personal vision. Life could be harsh, loud and wrong as it wished,

but they lived it fully, and when they expressed their attitude
toward the world it was with a fluid style that reduced the chaos
of living to form.[57]

Jazz reduces the "chaos of living to form." The effect of this transformation can be profound. According to Neil Leonard, pianist Mary
Lou Williams occasionally interrupted her performances to implore
inattentive audiences, "Listen, this will heal you."[58]

In learning from jazz, it is important to recognize the pitfalls in
many interpretations of jazz by white critics. The role of racism in the
lives of jazz artists and in the economic exploitation of black artists
must not be overlooked. Jazz is born from a complex mix of creativity
and persistence, of living outside of and in defiance of the stifling man-
tle of racism.[59] I find it ironic, and yet fitting, that we who are white
can also find in jazz resources for creating identities as Americans outside of racism.

Jazz has a complex development that is destroyed by describing
jazz history in terms of beginnings, stages, and types. Much of that
definition by white critics is challenged by jazz artists. The linear story
that focuses on great composers and innovative geniuses is misleading,
as is the very notion of linear developments.[60] In my references to jazz,
what I find thought provoking about it is precisely the way jazz
escapes neat categories, the ranking of performers and schools, a narrative of progress and linear developments.

White critics have also misunderstood jazz by seeing it only in
terms of an experience of excess, emotion, and ecstasy. Jazz is often
described as basically primitive, emotional, physical, sexual, and ecstatic. In some cases jazz is disparaged for possessing these qualities, in
others it is romanticized. The only difference is whether that excess is
valued and celebrated and seen as ecstasy, or disparaged as excess and
hysteria. But as Gabbard states, in either case, the world view is the
same. In both cases jazz remains safely "other," the production of people who are not us: "But whether the music was demonized or romanticized, the result was the same: jazz was the safely contained world of
the Other where whites knew they could find experiences unavailable
to them at home."[61]

In contrast to these interpretations of jazz as entertainment—superb entertainment, ecstatic entertainment, but mere entertainment nonetheless—I claim that jazz is intellectual, physical, and ecstatic. Far from being a primitive form of expression, jazz is intellectually challenging, sensual, and viscerally transformative. Listening to jazz brings pleasure and rewards intense attention. I look at jazz not as antithetical to critical thinking but as an intensely pleasurable and challenging component of creative ethical reflection and political strategizing. I claim that listening to jazz helps us feel in nondualistic ways, brings pleasure in nondualistic ways, and therefore helps us think, act, and respond in different and nondualistic ways.

Contrast the power and pleasure of jazz with the power and pleasure of the music of Richard Wagner. As Bernard Holland notes in his critical evaluation of the performance of the *Ring of the Nibelung* by the Metropolitan Opera House, "Richard Wagner predicted that his music would drive men mad. It did, and it does. Other composers thrill, sadden, exalt, bore, irritate or amuse. Wagner arouses feelings that alarm us about ourselves."[62] Holland does not make the facile claim that Wagner's music causes fascism, but in recounting the support of Wagner's family for Hitler, he points to the coincidence of energy, violence, desire and pleasure in "the music of one (Wagner) and the politics of the other (Hitler)."[63]

> Wagner and Hitler bypass civilization: they appeal to something deeper in us, something violent, sensual, yearning, acquisitive, and in the case of Wagner, pleasurable beyond measure. All the primitive impulses humankind has tried to forget are revived in the music of one and the politics of the other.[64]

Holland also speaks of the appeal of the music of Wagner and the politics of Hitler for many Germans: "The Germans, aching to fulfill ancient destinies, certain of the power of their origins, must have felt something much the same as they embraced their 'blessed Adolf'."[65]

Jazz offers another sort of pleasure, another awakening of vitality, sensuality, intellectual energy, and will. In contrast to the politics and art of violence, ancient destinies and inevitable victory, in jazz and the blues we find the power and pleasure of 'virtuosity in the face of limits,' the power and joy of holding together seemingly intractable oppositions (suffering, rage, hope, and determination), all without illusions of simple or final answers.

Think about the logic of jazz. Jazz emerges from the interplay of structure and improvisation, collectivity and individuality, tradition and innovation. What goes on when jazz is performed? Jazz is not completely free form. There are standards, songs that can be played again and again. The score of jazz ranges from a chord progression and melody, to a full orchestration with openings for improvisation. From that core, the players innovate and improvise, modifying the chords, melodies, and rhythm. The pleasure and energy of jazz comes from hearing both a familiar chord progression and melody and the new possibilities, what can be done from that structure. The ability to improvise is fueled both by individual effort, creativity, and technique and by group synergy: the technical skill and creativity of each player is as foundational as is the spark that comes from playing off of each other.

What does it take to improvise? A key element is respect for the tradition, learning from it without merely repeating it. This respect is expressed by Miles Davis: "I played 'My Funny Valentine' for a long time—and didn't like it—and all of a sudden it meant something."[66] Another essential element in jazz is respect for other players. As James Collier emphasizes, the worst that can be said of a jazz player is that he or she doesn't listen.[67] A third element is an openness to learning something new from an old piece and from other players, working with difference and novelty. Amiri Baraka highlights this aspect of jazz in his description of the playing of Chico Freeman: "He can unleash all the fire and mystery and otherness of the outside, but within the unifying and compelling vision of the carefully made. And this is what we look for, what we listen for, in any genre or style, the care and attention of the skilled craftsman along with the fire and passion of the exquisitely sensitive."[68] And what is evoked by the performance of jazz? Joy, energy, and intellectual challenge for both players and listeners. Eric Lott sees this dimension of jazz in the playing of Charlie Parker: "Jazz was a struggle which pitted mind against the perversity of circumstance, and . . . in this struggle blinding virtuosity was the best weapon."[69]

Miller cites the claim of Deleuze that Foucault was trying to change his way of thinking from "a vitalism founded on mortalism, preoccupied with death in its singular negativity as the defining moment of existence, to a vitalism founded, instead, on aesthetics—that is, on an understanding of life, in its positivity, as a unique pattern of acts and ideas that, like a work of art, one might fashion for oneself."[70]

Jazz *is* a vitalism founded on aesthetics; on creativity, integrity, and energy in the face of societal limits; and on individual failures, limits, and mistakes. Bob Blumenthal claims that jazz emerges from the awareness of who the other musicians are, what they are doing at this moment, and their particular configuration of strengths and weaknesses. Niels-Henning Ørsted identified this awareness as central to the creativity of Oscar Peterson: "What Oscar is doing . . . is using people to do the best of what *they* can do."[71]

This awareness includes acknowledging and working with mistakes and limitations. Note Joel Siegel's assessment of what made Billie Holiday the "greatest singer in jazz history":

> Even in her youth, Holiday's voice was not, in itself, remarkable. Compared to Ella Fitzgerald and Sarah Vaughan, she possessed a limited instrument—relatively narrow in range, tone and color. The way Holiday used her voice—her resourceful alterations of melody; her dramatic, often ironic approach to lyrics; her peerless sense of swing—is what made her the greatest singer in jazz history, inspiring several generations of artists. . . .
>
> In her later recordings, Holiday compensated for the deterioration of her voice by delving deeper into the emotional content of her songs.[72]

Not all limits are seen, not all are easily compensated for. There are failures in jazz.[73] Jeff Rosen describes one such failure in a form not noted for critique, the liner notes to a set of recordings by Miles Davis and John Coltrane:

> This diversity doesn't always work as well. "Fran Dance," Miles' reworking of the dance tune "Put Your Little Foot Right

Out," suffers a bit from the soloists' different conceptions. Miles, playing with his harmon mute right up against the microphone, creates a delicate and fragile mood which is shattered by Adderley's bluesy solos and Trane's explosive harmonies.[74]

Benny Green, in his tribute to the art of Billie Holiday, claimed that jazz operates at the "knife-edge of failure."[75] Humphrey Littleton claimed that part of the power of Louis Armstrong's work was his ability to "overcome and glorify unimaginative backing," and "to recover from a bad mistake and continue on his way without the missing of a beat."[76] Bill Evans claimed that "in jazz, a mistake can be—in fact, must be—justified by what follows it."[77] There are mistakes in jazz; mistakes that come from a failure of imagination, lack of skill, a failure to listen carefully to the other musicians, mistakes that come, not from the energy of transgression, but from the energy of pushing the limit, what Sidney Bechet called "playing ahead of themselves" and Miles Davis called getting musicians "to go beyond themselves".[78]

> If you put a musician in a place where he has to do something different from what he does all the time, then he can do that— but he's got to think differently in order to do it. He has to use his imagination, be more creative, more innovative; he's got to take more risks. He's got to play above what he knows—far above it—and what that might lead to might take him above the place where he's been playing all along, to the new place where he finds himself right now—and to the next place he's going and even above that! . . . I've always told the musicians in my band to play what they *know* and then play *above that*. Because then anything can happen, and that's where great art and music happen.[79]

The result can be exhilarating and frustrating. Art Blakey describes the pleasure of taking risks: "Jazz is not clinical. . . . Jazz is born by somebody goofin'. So if you feel that band hasn't got that looseness, they're not creating."[80] Wynton Marsalis offers another perspective on the competition that is part of jazz, and what happens when you don't measure up: "No matter what anybody says, nobody wants their head served to them. . . . It has happened to everybody, and nobody likes it."[81] Teddy Edwards also describes the competition of jazz, and the response of seasoned musicians to the mix of success and failure:

> You trade ideas and see if you can come up to the level.... Sometimes you fall short. It's a funny thing, one night it would be my night, the next Dexter's or Lucky Thompson's or Wardell's. Whatever happened, the next day you got up, put on a pot of beans and practiced all day.[82]

What does it mean to participate in this play of creativity alongside the "knife-edge of failure" and the pleasure of "goofin"? What is the drive? Dizzy Gillespie described it as the search for truth.

> "I did an interview with Dizzy Gillespie once in Cuba," Chico [Freeman] recalls, "and the guy asks one of those questions you've heard 275 times and it *still* doesn't make a lot of sense; he asks, 'What is jazz?' Well, Dizzy answered the question right away. He said jazz is the search for truth. And as soon as he said that, the light went on, and I added, 'And truth is what *is*'—not what was, or what will be. Truth is in the moment. To play who or what you are *at that moment*—that's a skill that has to be developed in all musicians.... And there's a certain serenity that comes from simply being who you really are."[83]

To play who we are at this moment, what does this mean for us in our work for justice? At times, in the midst of our multiform political efforts, our intersecting yet individual efforts at establishing justice, we respect each other and listen deeply to each other. We may then be sparked by the boldness and insight of others, by other communities, by others within our own community—inspired not to replicate their efforts, but to act with a similar degree of boldness, energy, and expertise.

Our communities can have the power and fluidity of jazz. This happens as we focus not just on particular strategies for social justice but also on what creates those policies and strategies—the values, connection, and community from which questions, analyses, strategies, and policies emerge, answers that are right for a time but that can be criticized and re-evaluated.

For some, this connection is grounded in faith. For many Jews and Christians community is grounded in a narrative of being in a relationship with God and with other people who are created in the image of God. Thus the basis of welfare reform is compassion and respect, not merely technocratic and bureaucratic concerns or attempts to mollify a strident and troublesome constituency. For those of us who aren't theists, the connection that founds our community is humanistic: the substance of our narrative is the joy, chaos, and energy of creative work with other people and with nature.

Let's stay with the analogy of jazz. What is the chord progression for a cohesive community? Respect for every human being; commitment to justice; self-criticism; an awareness of our own weaknesses and flaws; openness to conflict, critique, and change; compassion; energy; creativity; delight in the surprise and unexpected gifts of life.

There is another element to the chord progression of cohesive and self-critical community that I have learned from the logic of jazz. The ground of social critique and transformation is not the ideal versus the real but the real versus the real. Remember Charlie Parker and virtuosity in the face of limits: we resist the reality of greed, exploitation, and indifference because of the reality of compassion, respect, and deep-seated and long-lasting commitment to social justice.

Think back to the challenges that face us in our political work—competing analyses of the root causes of current forms of exploitation and injustice, mutually exclusive strategies, fragile and fractious coalitions, all exacerbated by internal divisions and power struggles. In the past, I would have interpreted these errors or limits as due to oppression and as being somehow remediable. Now I see them, as far we can imagine, as being as likely to be constitutive as accidental. I am intrigued by the notion that our strengths carry with them their flaws and weaknesses. My interpretation of this is not, however, tragic, cynical, or pessimistic. How do we acknowledge our limits and our complicity without despair, without cynicism, and, most importantly, *without humility*? Let's look at this like a jazz musician. How do we bounce off these strengths and weaknesses? How do we play up the strengths and at the same time check and limit the corrosive effects of the weaknesses?

Note that I did not say eradicate the weakness. Here is my wager: the innovation, creativity, power, precision, beauty, and responsiveness that heal and affect people's lives, our lives, in positive ways may emerge as readily from our acknowledgment and check to each others' constitutive weaknesses as from building on each others' strengths. There is a story, possibly apocryphal, that one jazz artist, when asked where he came up with the ideas for such original improvisations, said that it came from having to do something with the other musicians' mistakes.

I am proposing a simple change in vision. Rather than denouncing or bemoaning the partiality and weakness of others' responses, let us see them as something to be responded to, played with, and worked with.

Where does this leave us in our work for justice, in our attempts to build and sustain community?

We are not ushering in a new age.

We are not part of a grand cultural revolution.

We are not fighting the war to end all wars.

We are, quite simply, like all the generations before us, and all the generations that will come after, learning to walk.

Jon Poses' description of the improvisation and compositions of the jazz pianist Joanne Brackeen serves as an image of what communal work for justice can be:

> And, as is always the case with Brackeen's music, each piece she delivers serves as a musical adventure, a kind of joyous, non-clichéd, feast-filled, self-sustaining entity with unpredictable passages, uncommon angles, unexpected energy pockets and stops and starts that house circular and centrifugal motion."[84]

Our communities, our work for justice, can be as audacious as the compositions of Joanne Brackeen. As we listen to each other, as we are open to seeing and playing off our limits and strengths, weaknesses and possibilities, what happens with all of our strategies, our coalitions, our communities, even our work for justice? It swings.

2

"FRUSTRATION AND RIGHTEOUS ANGER DO NOT A POLITICS MAKE"*

—Glenn C. Loury, "Across the Great Divide"

One of the most disorienting things that can happen to a radical critic of patriarchal, authoritarian, racist, and elitist power structures is to win. It is often quite a shock to move from the pure energy of unrelenting and uncompromising critique of unjust structures to the more complex task of shaping institutions. The difficulties of building coalitions, of mobilizing financial resources, of proposing, implementing and then evaluating specific policies are exacerbated if our critiques and our visions of justice are shaped by dualistic images of good and evil and by delusions of our own relative innocence.

Along with many feminists of my generation, I once assumed that women would be better at using political and economic power than men. It may well be argued that women as a group do less harm than

*"Across the Great Divide: new calls for understanding and reconciliation from two venerable warriors on behalf of racial justice," Glenn Loury, *New York Times Book Review,* June 23, 1996, pg. 11.

27

men. We are not the majority of generals, presidents, corporate executives, or directors of the International Monetary Fund and major banks. Do we do less harm, however, because we are morally superior, or because we have less power?

I propose that women do less harm only because we have less power.[1] Once we gain power, it becomes clear that we are as inept in using it fairly as men. Our failures are not necessarily the same as those of men, but they are failures nonetheless.

Let me be more specific. One of the greatest traumas in gaining power is seeing the social costs of what at the personal level were mere eccentricities or foibles. Weaknesses and flaws in character, when expressed between friends and family, may be annoying (avoiding conflict, telling only part of the truth, or "innocent" lies in the interest of social harmony, seeking an inordinate amount of control in relation to other people) but they are rarely politically destructive. Once an individual gains power, however, once a group gains power, the impact of those foibles is magnified.

There is nothing like gaining leadership to shatter illusions of self-righteousness, of pure motives, of having the decisive analyses and the correct strategies. The opportunity for those of us who have been marginalized to abuse power emerges when we gain power either by becoming insiders in a formerly criticized institution, or as our movements for social change gain in numbers and political influence. I contend that it is easier to check the internal power struggles of opposition movements, easier to check our own abuses of power once we are on the inside, if we have a nondualistic image of good and evil.[2] If our views of justice, of truth, of order are shaped by a dualistic logic in which there is a clear division between good and evil, truth and error, order and chaos, purity and corruption, commitment to the greater good and mere self-aggrandizement, then we are likely to be shattered by abuses of power, disillusioned when we see it in others, defensive and resistant to criticism when others see it in us.

I am wary, therefore, of any sort of vanguard consciousness, be it that of the Christian Right, the proletariat, or even the experiences of feminist women. I am a feminist, proud to be part of this movement for the full humanity of women. My feminist identity is not, however, uncritical, but is itself the ground of my critique of feminism as well as my critique of other communities and movements.

It often seems that to value our communities, to have pride in our identities as Christians, as humanists, as feminists, as American, as white, means that we have to think that our community is, if not unambiguously, at least overwhelmingly on the side of right; if not unambiguously good and praiseworthy, at least predominantly so, its legacy more one of opportunity and justice than one of exploitation and coercion. In my work in multicultural education, I try to help people and communities develop a more complex sense of identity, one that incorporates both pride and accountability.

The reason for this dual focus is simple: my own experience of a community that values and learns from difference, and my own immersion in a community that denies and demonizes difference, is the same: it is my work with other feminists for social justice. At times, the women's movement has been a place where we have analyzed and learned from the diverse experiences of women. It has been a place where we have explored the strengths that we have that transcend female stereotypes of passivity and emotionality, valuing our work as leaders and as scholars.[3]

And yet, at other times, we have turned on each other, threatened by our differences, fearful of the otherness that exists among even feminist women, denouncing as nonfeminist those women who have differing analyses of sexism and of its correlation with racism and class exploitation, denouncing those women who have different strategies for responding to bias, discrimination, and exploitation. We often find it much easier to denounce patriarchal structures than to work together, with other women and with men, to build equitable structures and institutions.[4]

Many of us have not learned how to resolve our conflicts—our friendships end, our coalitions shatter, when conflict emerges. Many of us do not know how to work together once we have serious disagreements. Our feminist communities, while ostensibly ones of support and cooperation, are often dependent on uniformity and agreement.[5]

I would like to tell you a funny story. In the mid-1970s, the women's movement caught fire in the United States and Europe. We began organizing with power and passion. Women claimed as ours the equal rights promised in the constitution and moved to challenge barriers to those rights. There was a vigorous campaign for an Equal Rights Amendment, and, in the absence of such a constitutional guarantee of equal rights, we used the clout present in existing laws to challenge discrimination in employment, in obtaining credit, in access to education. We fought in the courts and legislatures for reproductive freedom. We began to take seriously violence against women as a social and individual problem, organizing rape crisis centers and shelters for battered women, and developing legislation in regard to domestic violence and rape that recognized the insights of women and the serious nature of these assaults.[6]

As we gained access to educational institutions, we began questioning the cultural assumptions that perpetuated the oppression of women. From the vantage point of women's experience, we criticized the false universalism of Enlightenment humanism and Christian faith, we questioned the false inclusivity of Christianity, Judaism, and Islam.[7]

Now here's the funny part. As we developed strong and politically efficacious critiques of Enlightenment humanism and the partial inclusivity of religious traditions, we heard our understandings of women's experience criticized on all sides; as inadequate to interactions of race and gender, by women of color; as maintaining heterosexual assumptions, by lesbians; as reflecting class privilege, by working-class women; as reinforcing the very notions we sought to dismantle by the way we were using the concepts of gender, sex, and women's experience; and, not the least significant, rejected by many women who disavowed feminism and said we did not speak for them or understand their reality.[8]

Such turmoil over using three basic concepts: women, experience, and the claim that the personal is the political.

As we have worked with these categories, all three have been valuable in making major changes in the lives of women. All three have also been found to be limited and are criticized as being as falsely universal as the Enlightenment humanism and religious anthropolgies we sought to replace.

I am not going to rehearse this debate in detail. Nor am I going to resolve it. I am going to provide another way of looking at it, assessing its meaning and participating in it.

The appeal to women's experience has worked as a powerful hermeneutic and lever in political action because it has been erroneously viewed as a metaphysical claim—saying something real, true, and universal about women. The appeal to women's experience has been politically effective and the source of theoretical insight as much because it is "wrong" as because it is "right." It has been a powerful catalyst for social change—not in spite of its political limits and theoretical errors, but through those errors.

Some feminists dismiss the appeal to women's experience because of its partiality—saying it has been used to universalize the experience of white, middle- to upper-class women, thus perpetuating the same forms of exclusion as Enlightenment humanism or religious anthropologies.[9] There is another interpretation—the turn to women's experience can be seen as a hermeneutic, as a way of asking questions, and not as a metaphysical claim, a final description of how things are.[10] White women's descriptions of our experience have elicited challenges to that description. Women of color have not rejected the appeal to women's experience per se. They have, rather, entered the debate, by describing their experiences and basing theoretical analyses and political strategizing on those experiences.[11]

While it is easy, in principle, to accept the intrinsic expansiveness of the appeal to women's experience, the concrete results of that appeal have been painful, frightening and disruptive. Why has this inclusion of an unfolding range of experiences been resisted, and why has pointing out the inevitable particularity of women's experience been seen as an indictment? Why has it been so hard for white feminists to hear how our being is as constituted by race and class as by gender?[12]

As white feminists, we have been seeking "innocent knowledge." Our indictment of patriarchy and our constructive work have all been framed in a dualistic logic of truth and error, victims and oppressors. Since we have condemned patriarchal modes of thought for excluding us, it is hard when we are charged with being as exclusive of other women. It is as though we cannot imagine being at the same time a victim of sexism and a perpetrator of racism. Also, given our rejection of masculine exclusion as deliberate, it is hard to find ourselves criticized on similar grounds. If we are also capable of exclusion, discrimination, and oppression, on what basis do we claim power, on what basis can we act?

Behind this dismay and fear is the illusion that there is "innocent knowledge" to be had—that as women, we have a vantage point that can expose injustice but not perpetuate it. As feminists, it is difficult to acknowledge that our analyses and projects for social justice are as partial and marked by power differences as are the analyses of the Enlightenment and religious traditions.

Jane Flax describes this problem well. She criticizes the longing for "innocent knowledge" and its effects in feminist theory. By "innocent knowledge," Flax means "the discovery of some sort of truth which can tell us how to act in the world in ways that benefit or are for the (at least ultimate) good of all. Those whose actions are grounded in or informed by such truth will also have *their* innocence guaranteed. They can only do good, not harm to others. They act as the servant of something higher and outside (or more than) themselves, their own desires and the effects of their particular histories or social locations."[13]

What is wrong with such a goal? Surely it is praiseworthy to try to do good, to find checks to our own desires and correctives to the limits of our vision. The problem with the search for innocent knowledge is that our efforts at knowing fully and acting justly are not only contextual, but also inevitably partial and flawed, a mixture of our own will to power and a genuine commitment to justice and freedom.

Flax claims that the ability to see the ways in which given systems of knowing, valuing, and acting are shaped by relationships of power (e.g., racism, sexism, class privilege, homophobia) does not mean that we have escaped situatedness, fallibility, desire, and self-interest. To see how another's system of reason maintains his social power does not mean that ours does not do the same thing.

As Flax argues, this applies even to the feminist concept of gender. Gender is our concept: it helps us see patterns of domination and it gives us political power by providing a leverage for political organizing and social change. It is a powerful concept, a helpful concept—and a limited concept.

> Gender has been reconceived as a highly variable and historically contingent set of human practices. Gender relations pervade many aspects of human experience from the constitution of the "inner self" and family life to the so-called public worlds of the state, the economy, and knowledge production. Gender is not a stable thing; it is certainly not a set of anatomical or biological attributes, although the relation of gender to embodiment is an interesting and controversial question among feminist theorists. We cannot even claim that gender is a universal or unitary relation present in all cultures, because it is a category that feminist theorists have constructed to analyze certain relations in our cultures and experiences. The concept must therefore reflect our questions, desires, and needs.[14]

Similarly, a postmodern critique is as much an exercise of power as it is a critique of power. We do gain influence and energy from exposing as pretensions claims to clarity, univocal truth, and absolute justice.

I am more surprised by the vehemence of some postmodern critiques of the partiality and embeddedness of feminist analyses. Why the shock? Why the outrage? What else could our thought be? Our language, our concepts, our symbols, our rituals, our practices are all historical, all embedded, all shaped by relationships of care, respect, and domination.

Tracy Chapman's recent song *"Let's Start Over,"* manifests such a longing for purity and justice. Yet the very longing for categories that are unambiguous is itself part of the logic of domination, the illusion that imperfection and error are solely negative and not part of the ingredients of creativity. We do not reach "truth" by transcending error, by defeating enemies, by containing chaos; we do not reach "truth" in spite of our particularity, our frailty, our finitude. We reach "truth" through error, through chaos, through responding to cruelty and exploitation.

All our knowing and acting is partial. We see, plan, think, and feel through categories that are both disclosive and limited. If we give up the claim or pretension of innocent knowledge, a different strategy and response is opened. Here are my assumptions and guidelines. As a postmodern theorist, I have two absolutes. First, I can be wrong, as can every system of thought, every community, every movement, every group of people that I trust. We can be wrong not just in the sense of being partial in our analyses and ineffective in our strategies, but also by being immoral, corrupt, short-sighted, and self-serving. What makes this a postmodern ethos and not a tragic ethos is that I see these errors and moral flaws as being ironic, humorous, and the spur to greater creativity. My second absolute: under conditions of justice, life is deeply rewarding, meaningful, and joyous. Even taking risks for further justice is more an act of self and community affirmation than sacrifice. In contrast to Foucault, my work is grounded in the reality, not just of happiness, but of happiness *and* joy.

Given these two absolutes, there are three criteria for the truthfulness of our analyses and strategies: (1) their actual effect in the lives of people, (2) their openness to further critique and hence modification, and (3) their resiliency in the face both of critique and unintended consequences—positive and negative, unpredictable opportunities for further acts of responsibility and creativity.

There is an alternative if we give up our search for innocent subjectivity just as we give up the illusion of innocent knowledge. Let's look at our identities as women like a jazz artist. That riff, the cultural construction of gender, has had widely varying and mutually exclusive effects—at times the gender division has been destructive, maintained through violence, women used primarily for male pleasure and fulfillment. At other times there has been more power between separated genders. Also, some activists have created powerful riffs by using the category of gender—women gathering together for critique and creativity—and seeing through our work together both the costs of the construct of gender, the costs of that division between male and female, and finding in work with each other support for shaping different institutions and different ways of being human.

I think it is possible to admire the virtuosity with which some play the categories of gender (take, for example, Mary McClintock Fulkerson's analysis of the different understandings of gender, subjectivity, and agency in Appalachian women, Presbyterian laywomen, and feminist academic theologians.)[15] I think it is also possible to criticize uses of the category of gender to control and exploit. What I do not think possible is the formulation of categories of gender—ways of speaking of identity, agency, relationships between self and other, between self and community—without the potential for harm and control. We look for better categories, those most fitting and evocative, not final categories, realizing that even our "better" categories are likely to be shaped not only by partiality but also by traces of domination and control.

There is a nondualistic logic, a nondualistic way of understanding power, moral agency, and social critique. I turn now to the work of Theophus Smith and his analysis of conjure to describe a nondualistic image of religious and political power, and to the work of Karen McCarthy Brown to describe a nondualistic image of moral agency.

When we have the power to shape our institutions, how do we grasp this opportunity and utilize it effectively? The challenge is most basically one of practices, not of ideas. In his recent book, *Conjuring Culture,* Theophus Smith provides a framework for examining the interaction of religious and political life. He takes the notion of conjure and uses it to highlight the intrinsically religious and political dimensions of social transformation in African American life. Conjure involves eliciting spiritual power, transforming internalized oppression, evoking and sustaining acts of political transformation through a complex interaction of religious symbol systems, ritual performances, and political actions. Conjure describes the healing of an entire people, a challenge to systems of domination. Smith analyzes "cultural performances that involve curative transformations of reality by means of mimetic operations and processes."[16] Conjure "encompasses social-historical transformations as well as folklore practices."[17]

> I refer to such transformations as instances of conjuring culture, specifically where I find (1) ritually patterned behaviors and performative uses of language and symbols (2) conveying a pharmacopeic or healing/harming intent and (3) employing bib-

lical figures and issuing in biblical configurations of cultural experience.[18]

In his work, Smith analyzes instances of conjure and explores the need for further conjurational practices by African Americans. His book also raises a sharp challenge to Euro-Americans. We, too, are certainly in need of healing: healing from the deadly constructions of whiteness as domination, healing from identity formations that mask complicity with oppression while simultaneously eliciting such oppression. Smith does not apply "conjure" to the spiritual-political-cultural dimensions of Euro-American religion, for we lack a systematic integration of material work, political activism, and spiritual practice. Smith states that he "reserves the term conjure" "for African American transformations because of their more clearly articulated pharmacopeic, ritual and magical orientations."[19] What we Euro-Americans need, however, are practices that are explicitly conjurations of freedom, freedom from domination, freedom for risk, freedom from constructions of virtue and responsibility as control.

How do we conjure our way out of domination? Smith offers a key ingredient in his very definition of conjure. By definition, conjure escapes the dualistic oppositions of good and evil, sacred and profane. Working with the notion of the pharmokos, he reminds us that that which heals, can also harm.

> Concisely stated, conjure is not only sorcery or witchcraft but also a tradition of healing and harming that transforms reality through performances and processes involving a mimetic use of medicinal and toxic substances.[20]

Citing Raboteau, Smith reminds us that "we should be careful not to collapse the defensive and offensive distinction into the moral dichotomy of good versus evil." That is to say, "offensive conjure can be good as well as defensive conjure, and either can be malign."[21] It is this denial of the coincidence of good and evil, of help and harm, that is an intrinsic aspect of the evocation of domination and enmity. People who locate evil and harm primarily in someone else, be it the benighted masses or the heretical enemy, miss their own complicity in systems of oppression, often fail to see the possibilities for transformation in the enemy, and find a justification for the exclusion or domination of the enemy.[22]

What does this mean for groups working for social justice? What are our habits, how do we attend to our "enemies," those on the outside, those on the "inside" who are getting in the way of "truly effective work" because of their commitment to the "wrong" strategy or persistence in the "wrong" analysis? How do we work with our own proclivities toward self-interest and the abuse of power? How do we move with the chaos and conflicts that accompany group decision making and institutional change? I contend that looking at these habits provides clues to understanding how we defeat ourselves, how it is that internal political struggles become deadly rather than simply being part of the necessary process of working with other people.

I have found two sources especially helpful in describing typical and problematic habits of self- and other-regard, habits of viewing ambiguity and opposition, that often occur in groups. Both writers focus on the concrete process of making effective decisions in certain limited situations. Rosabeth Moss Kanter's book is based on her study of decision making and change within major U.S. corporations. Gary Oxenhandler's essay is based on his work as a practicing attorney, conferring with clients, participating in committees, working with people in situations in which decisions have to be made and negotiation with an actual or potential adversary is necessary. Oxenhandler, in his description of "the dynamics that drive groups and individuals in their decision making," and Kanter, in her analysis of the "art and architecture" of institutional change, provide glimpses into the complex web of ethical and theological assumptions, habits, and dispositions that I claim are intrinsic aspects of a culture of domination.[23]

Oxenhandler and Kanter are focused on practice: what attitudes, questions, and assumptions can help individuals and groups make decisions more effectively? In their divergent accounts of effective decision making, I claim that we can find the resonance of nondualistic habits, habits of self-definition, habits of viewing the other, habits of seeing, naming, and responding to the complex of "good and evil," better and worse, right and wrong, effective and ineffective.

Oxenhandler describes the "mental posturing" that "all of us *initially* take when decision making involves opposition or an adversary":

> I am invulnerable.
> I am psychologically stronger than my adversary.
> I am financially stronger than my adversary.
> I am a better negotiator than my adversary.
> I have the best advice and I am listening to it.
> I am right and my adversary is wrong.
> God is on my side.
> I will win and my adversary will lose. [24]

Those of us whose identities are shaped by both privilege and exclusion may not be able to make all of these assumptions (few women would claim invulnerability or greater financial strength, for instance), but we can make enough of them to find ourselves manifesting the illusions of what Oxenhandler calls SelfConsensus. In his description of SelfConsensus, Oxenhandler builds on Janus's analysis of GroupThink. SelfConsensus is the process by which we "positively reinforce our own conclusions so as to convince ourselves that we are right," and this process shares with GroupThink a complex of illusions. Janus describes eight illusions of GroupThink, two of which are especially pertinent for our purposes: "An unquestioned belief in the group's inherent morality, inclining the members to ignore the ethical or moral consequences of their decision," and "direct pressure on any member who expresses strong arguments against any of the group's stereotypes, illusions or commitments, making clear that this type of dissent is contrary to what is expected of all loyal members". [25]

Kanter describes a similar process at work in the "art and architecture of change." [26] She notes that there is often a clear disjunction between the institutional memory of change and the process of change itself. While the memory of change focuses on clarity, certainty, rightness, and consensus, the process of change is characterized by conflict, risk, errors, and confusion.

Where groups or organizations appear to "act," there are often strong individuals persistently pushing.

Where recent events seem the most important in really bringing the change about, a number of less obvious early events were probably highly important.

Where there is apparent consensus, there was often controversy, dissent, and bargaining.

Where the ultimate choice seems the only logical one, unfolding naturally and inevitably from what precedes it, there were often a number of equally plausible alternatives that might have fitted too.

Where clear-sighted strategies are formulated, there was often a period of uncertainty and confusion, of experiment and reaching for anyone with an answer, and there may have been some unplanned events or "accidents" that helped the strategy to emerge.

Where single leaders or single occurrences appear to be the "Cause" of the change, there were usually many actors or many events.

Where an innovation appears to have taken hold, there may be contradictory tendencies in the organization that can destroy or replace it, unless other things have occurred to solidify—institutionalize—the change.

And where there appears to be only continuity, there was probably also change.

Where there appears to be only change, there was probably also continuity. [27]

According to Kanter, those who master change must know and understand the conflictual and chaotic processes of change, but they must also utilize and create dualistic myths that deny that very process. She argues that "change masters" create myths in which "conflicts disappear into consensuses," "equally plausible alternatives disappear into obvious choices," and "accidents, uncertainties, and muddle-headed confusions disappear into clear-sighted strategies" and "the fragility of changes (that exist alongside the residues of the old system) disappear into images of solidity and full actuality."[28] She claims that

> to get commitment and support for a course of action may
> require that it appear essential—not as one of a number of possi-
> bilities. By the time a decision is announced, it may need to be
> presented as the only choice, even if there are many people
> aware of how much debate went into it or how many other
> options looked just as good. The … champions of the idea—
> have to look unwaveringly convinced of the rightness of their
> choice to get other people to accept the change.[29]

Kanter assumes as inevitable, and even productive, an intrinsically
hierarchical situation: there are those who engineer change, and those
who are affected by it. Those who engineer change understand the
complexity of the change process, but they use dualistic myths of clarity, consensus, and certainty to gain assent. As Kanter states, "those
who master change know that they can never tell the 'truth,' but they
also know what the 'truth' is."[30]

Contrast Kanter's change master with Oxenhandler's deliberate challenge to illusions of certainty, morality, invulnerability, and
success:

> Always, always, always bear in mind that you *are* vulnerable;
> that your adversary *may be* psychologically and financially
> stronger than you; that although you *may be* getting the best
> advice, you *may not be* listening to it; that you *may not be* right;
> that everyone has their own God (and that even though your
> God is on your side, your adversary's God may be on their side
> and may be more powerful than your God); and, that you *may
> not* win.[31]

Oxenhandler's model strikes at the heart of the illusions necessary
for domination—certainty of both power and the right to use that
power, security in the wisdom of one's own analyses, motives, and
plans. Kanter's model, however, has deep resonance with the founding
myths of western culture. Note the similarity between her change
master, successfully evoking myths of inevitable choices and wide-
spread consensus, with Weber's description of the charismatic political
leader, one who convinces his or her followers that they are at the very

heart of things, certain of eventual triumph, part of a process that is larger than the human agents who participate in it. Geertz, in his discussion of charisma, goes so far as to posit a necessary and intrinsic sacrality of central authority, a human need for the right answer and submission to a powerful leader who implements that right answer in political and cultural life.[32]

It is easy for us to see the danger of charismatic authority, of certainties of victory and rightness when they are held by our adversaries: we see the exclusion of dissent, the legitimation of violence against scapegoats, against those who obstruct and oppose the grand vision of society. I must admit, for example, that Newt Gingrich's promise "to bury any remains of what he disdainfully called the Great Society counterculture McGovernick legacy and return American to a more black and white view of right and wrong" makes *my* blood run cold.[33]

But what about the operation of this mindset among us—those of us on the Left, among feminists, progressives, those committed to work for racial justice? Do we not make the same mistakes, participate in the same error—so certain of our commitment to social justice that we assume that our strategies for attaining justice must also be right, pure, and untainted by error, illusion, and self-interest? Do we not also silence those who offer sharply divergent strategies for achieving equality and justice? I find that all too often our work for social change is marred by internal struggles over who is feminist enough or who is black enough—enforcing uniformity, being threatened by real differences all the while we sincerely and wholeheartedly want to celebrate and sustain difference in mutually challenging as well as supportive interactions.

This is the place where conjure is needed, where our habits of evoking and celebrating power, vitality, and energy fail us. I contend that Kanter's model is too dangerous and, while no strategy is free of toxic elements, too infected with the poison of domination to be useful. Domination is intrinsic to the myth of the change master: it assumes an elite that understands the complexity of change, and yet masks it from those affected by it, and from those who actually implement the change. It leads too easily to illusions of moral purity, and thus the sanctioning of violence against scapegoats endemic to Christian cultures. Theophus Smith describes this phenomenon well:

> A troubling aspect of Christian apocalyptic traditions in general can also be found in black American apocalyptic. In each case one finds a theological irony: the irony of a religion that espouses forgiveness and reconciliation, on the one hand, and yet harbors a vigorous hope for divine wrath and retribution on the other.[34]

We find in the Christian apocalyptic imagination a conjunction of protestations of universal love—love for all human beings, a desire to share the fruits of the gospel with all the earth, and, simultaneously, a desire for vengeance, a celebration of the wrath of God that destroys those who fail to accept the proffered message of love and reconciliation.[35] There is a logic here—the lie of certain truth only maintained by violence against those who remind us of the tenuousness of our claims to morality, truth, and victory.[36]

On the surface, Kanter's model of the change master and Geertz's model of sacred authority and certain purpose appear affirming of human dignity and strength. After all, they offer the myth of being right, of being on the winning side, of being wise and creative and engineering and implementing not merely a good idea but the best idea, the necessary way of organizing human society. They offer a chance to be unambiguously on the side of the angels. And yet, these seeming glorifications of human capacities in service to a legitimate authority or purpose mask a deep contempt for other people—a contempt expressed in the division between those who know the truth and those who are manipulated by myths, a contempt manifest in the scapegoat phenomenon and its exclusions and violence.

At first reading, Oxenhandler's model seems pessimistic, almost misanthropic. Here we find not glorification of human intelligence or wisdom, but a reminder of our capacity for self-deception, error, and illusion. Yet paradoxically, this mindset, when grounded in connection, manifests both deep respect for other human beings and, not coincidentally, the potential to counter the toxins of elitism and domination. Let me explain. To acknowledge one's limits includes acknowledging the limits of others, and it also includes acknowledging the potential wisdom and insights of others as well as of oneself. The tenor of this nondualistic form of respect is described most clearly by Buber in his account of what occurs in the relationship of I and Thou:

> Love is a cosmic force. For those who stand in it and behold in it, [people] emerge from their entanglement in busy-ness; and the good and the evil, the clever and the foolish, the beautiful and the ugly, one after another become actual and a You for them; that is, liberated, emerging into a unique confrontation. Exclusiveness comes into being miraculously again and again and now one can act, help, heal, educate, raise, redeem.[37]

Buber affirms humanity with our faults, with our illusions and self-deceptions. From this matrix of seeing ourselves as flawed—but without attributing to that flaw fall, shame, or guilt—there can emerge a nondualistic vocabulary of strength and weakness, of insight and deception—one that emphasizes accountability, not guilt, a sensibility that encompasses a good-humored recognition of the accidents, the surprises, the muddles that characterize our attempts to implement the good.

Is there room for passion for justice, for outrage, for commitment in a sensibility that acknowledges our vulnerability and capacity for error? It is difficult to imagine this sensibility, for much of our religious and political symbol systems are so precisely the contrary. We don't have to resort to "Onward Christian soldiers"; "Once to every man and nation" is enough. In our familiar hymns, as in our seemingly secular constructions of efficiency and success, we are shaped by the assumption that momentous choices—those that have theological as well as ethical and political import—are crystal clear, and that we can respond with truth, power, and majesty to the call for justice.

Can we find glimpses of another sensibility? I think so, I think it is there, pulsing in the rhythms of the blues, singing in the evocative prose of Toni Morrison. Theophus Smith cites Ralph Ellison's description of "the transformative nature of the blues: The blues is an impulse to keep the painful details and episodes of a brutal experience alive in one's aching consciousness, to finger its jagged edge, and to transcend it, not by the consolation of philosophy, but by squeezing from it a near-tragic, near-comic lyricism."[38]

In contrast, Smith also reminds us of James Baldwin's claim that for Euro-Americans, our music is either happy or sad—an emotional state that correlates deeply with illusions of victory and rightness: we're either right, successful, and happy; or wrong, defeated, and miserable. What the wisdom of the blues evokes is a very different awareness, one that cannot be described as either optimism or pessimism, and that most certainly is not adequately described as a tragic sense of life. Again, citing Jahnheinz Jahn, Smith highlights the homeopathic power of the blues, noting that "the melancholy is a camouflage."

> If we read the text of the blues songs without prejudice and notice the double meaning, which all authors emphasize, we find them mocking, sarcastic, tragi-comic, tragic, dramatic and accusing, often crudely humorous . . . [but] only exceptionally . . . melancholy.[39]

What would it mean for those of us shaped by the identity of dominance to embrace the spirituality and sensibility of the blues? We can stop taking ourselves too seriously so that we can respond, with utmost seriousness, to actual threats to human life. And in that response, we may remain fully aware of the limitations of our insight, our imaginations, and our courage. To move out of our identities as the dominant race, we must learn to fail—because we will, often and embarassingly and repeatedly. It is not easy to dismantle centuries-long structures of racial oppression, a self-definition predicated on racial divisions. And yet, as Myles Horton knew, and celebrates in his work *The Long Haul*, it is often in our failures that we learn the most, often in our failures that we discover deep ties with other people, in our failures that we plant the seeds of later victories.[40]

What religious sensibility can be conjured? What practices can emerge from this sensibility and then in turn sustain it ? We can be nourished by music that embodies the pain and the joy of work for justice, music that carries through tone, tenor, and rhythm the simultaneous hope for justice and a memory of the costs of oppression. We can be challenged and sustained by a spirituality that affirms our humanity as intrinsically capable of wisdom and error, kindness and self-centeredness, insight and self-delusions—without assuming that we'll ever be able to rid ourselves of the proclivity for error and harm.[41]

Another intimation of a nondualistic spirituality that can counter the toxins of domination is expressed in the poetry of Muriel Rukeyser:

> A miracle has even deeper roots,
> Something like failure, some profound defeat.
> Stumbled-over, the startle, the arousal,
> Something never perceived till now, the taproot.[42]

What is this taproot grasped only in failure, stumbled over in defeat and betrayal? It emerges in human connection: the resilience of our love for each other; the resilience of respect for ourselves and others in our illusions and error; the fact that in spite of, and even through our limitations, we are yet capable of kindness and compassion, and maybe at times even justice. And while those attempts are partial, as they will always be, the taproot is the courage and humor of a community that continues to learn, to love, to acknowledge our capacity for harm— and from that acknowledgment, to find together balm for the journey, presence and witness to the struggles and joys of life.

How do we actually work with our imperfections and failures without the enervation of humility, despair, or cynicism? I find a specific description of what a nondualistic form of moral agency might be, what it might actually be like for an individual and a community to operate with this notion of conjure, of healing power being both creative and destructive, in Karen McCarthy Brown's description of Haitian Vodou and the work of Mama Lola, or Alourdes. Karen McCarthy Brown states that Haitian Vodou is most decidedly a nondualistic world view, a religious and moral sensibility without a fall and without utopia: "From the Haitian perspective, there is no evidence that humans live in a fallen or imperfect state. There is no Golden Age in the past, no Utopia in the future."[43] The focus of moral energy, therefore, is not on defeating evil in some ultimate sense, either actually in history or ontologically, good having priority in the very nature of being. The focus of moral energy is learning to appreciate the richness of difference and conflict—within the self, between individuals. These differences are not easily understood, nor are conflicts always readily or smoothly resolved. Rather, "the point is not to make conflict go away but to make it work for, rather than against, life."[44] In this world view, the basic good is not the defeat of evil, but the maintenance of "high life energy and a strong sense of self balanced with responsiveness to others."[45]

Responsiveness to others does not always mean harmony. The very term "balance,"or "*balanse*" in vodou has a more dynamic sense. In order to attain responsiveness that is "good," responsiveness that is desired, that maintains high life energy, it is sometimes necessary to "set things reeling." "From this perspective it would seem that there is no essential evil assumed to reside within specific persons or within specific areas of the world. The moral problem is not evil but imbalance, both within and among persons."[46]

The way Karen McCarthy Brown describes the view of political power in vodou is quite similar to the understanding of power as conjure, a type of power that is neither essentially evil nor essentially good. Rather, power is intrinsically complex, and to understand power and to use it well it is a matter of balancing its complexity, of holding in mind its possible manifestations and noting what the possibilities of that power are in a specific situation.

Karen McCarthy Brown describes the lessons of power contained in activities of the Haitian spirit Ogou: "Ogou teaches that the power unleashed by human invention, unless ritually balanced, will turn on its creators."[47] How is this lesson conveyed? Brown describes the appearance of the warrior spirit Ogou, in the manifestation of Sin Jak Maje:

> Sin Jak's coming is marked with bravado.... [S]omeone brings
> out Sin Jak's sword.... He grabs it, unsheathes the blade and
> then thrusts it repeatedly in the air as if attacking an invisible
> enemy. Then, he lowers the blade and menacingly jabs it toward
> those standing nearest to him.... Finally, he points the blade at

himself. Resting the tip on his right hip, he pushes it in just enough to make the blade bend slightly—a gesture full of arrogance that hints at self-wounding.[48]

The lessons of power here are clear, and pertinent to those of us who see ourselves as marginalized or oppressed and justly criticizing the power of the oppressors. These lessons are rooted in the history of the Haitian republic, the successful slave revolt against the French in 1804, and the mixture of freedom and repression that has characterized Haitian politics.[49]

> Ogou repeats these lessons from history and keeps them alive in a variety of ways. Consider, for example, the ritualised gestures with the sword that we saw Sin Jak perform and that are frequently executed at the opening of the possession-performances of the other Ogou as well. The first gesture mimics attack on the enemy, the next threatens the immediate community, the final gesture points toward self-destruction.... Ogou's "dance" with the sword is to body language what proverbs are to spoken language: a condensation point for complex truths. Power liberates, power corrupts, power destroys.[50]

Does this mean that power is to be rejected? Does this mean that we can find a way of using power that is free of the possibility of corruption and destruction? Within the world view of Haitian Vodou, it is more appropriate to acknowledge the complexity of power, the ways in which "anger, wilfulness and assertion are at times essential, valuable, necessary ways of empower(ing) and restor(ing) dignity to those who face the 'enemy' daily, for example, in the humiliation of a trip to the welfare office."[51] And, yet, such power is not benign, not sanctified when it is used by those who are oppressed. "Ogou reminds his worshippers that the very same anger and self-assertive energy can be destructive when it is not properly balanced or aimed at the wrong target."[52]

The moral goal is not to find a pure form of power—say "power-with" rather than "power-over." The goal is participation in a ritual community that helps us see what type of power is needed, that helps us see if the power is properly balanced and properly directed.

The roles of the ritual community and of the spiritual leader are not to measure the moral worth of an individual or a community, but to help the individual and the community see what is going on, what the relationships of power are, and, from that seeing, find ways of balancing relationships and ways of balancing power: "What is reflected back to the viewer is a certain aspect of his or her life situation exaggerated for clarity and condensed into images that are easily retained. The Vodou participant does not turn to religion to be told what to do, but rather to be shown how to see."[53]

> In the West—that is in the European versions of Judaism and Christianity—a certain kind of thinking about religion and morality has been dominant. We feel that if we apply ourselves thoughtfully to our sacred texts and traditions, we can extract from them general principles that we can then hold up against our lives as measures of the moral quality to be found therein. The Vodou system is different. The relevant moral message does not measure a person's life so much as it reflects it.[54]

In the task of ritualized moral reflection, the moral leader serves as catalyst but not exemplar. Alourdes, for example, is not particularly "saintly." She is as capable of fault as any one else. Her role, her leadership, resides not in her superiority or her approach to perfection, but in her ability to initiate the process of reflection (which includes the community) in which there is a healing in "some disturbance in the networks of relations among people, often including a person's relationship to family members now dead."[55] Alourdes is not a leader because her behavior is to be emulated or imitated by others; she is, rather, "in charge of the process by which Vodou addresses moral dilemmas."[56]

Alourdes, under trance, is possessed by the spirits. The drama they enact requires, however, the participation of the entire community. The community is involved in the preparation of the ritual—the meal, the music, the dancing, the singing—that welcome the spirits, and the community is part of the interpretation of the message conveyed through the spirits. The performance of the spirits is ambiguous, and yet, according to Karen McCarthy Brown, this enriches the moral content, not compromises it. First, "the more conflict is present in the message, the more the community is galvanized into offering interpretations."[57] Thus the complex messages offered are matched in form by needing different human voices, different perspectives to interpret them.

In order to understand the catalytic work of Alourdes and the community, Karen McCarthy Brown describes the relationship between musical structure and social structure in Vodou. The musical structure is polyrhythmic; there are multiple rhythms at play, and the rhythm that unifies them is often absent, provided by those listening or by dancers. "No rhythm, not even the inner one, makes any musical sense in isolation. Meaning in African music arises from the mutual responsiveness of different rhythmic lines. For example, the dancers respond to the drummers and the drummers respond to the dancers. Drummers may shift their rhythmic patterning to match a particularly gifted dancer and then intensify it even further to urge her onto yet more energetic self-expression."[58]

The interpretation of ritual in Vodou is also multivalent: "The participant in a Vodou ritual must pour his or her own life content into the polymorphic interplay of images found there. Otherwise nothing will have meaning." When a ritual is successful, "everything comes together in such a way that what is going on within and among the people gathered there is expressed and clarified."[59]

The result is that a community and a self develop the ability to dance, to balance the polyrhythms of life. "A moral person ... is thus one who can balanse, 'dance,' in the midst of forces pulling in opposing directions without missing the beat."[60] This sense of self, this sense of morality, is intrinsically social: "The moral wisdom of Vodou lies in its teaching that it is precisely in responsive and responsible relation to others that one has the clearest and most steady sense of self."[61] This is not a morality of overcoming evil, of becoming sanctified, but rather of being fluid, open, responsive, able to see when one is misusing power, when one's community is abusing power, able to imagine other forms of relationship, able to find other rhythms, other ways of balancing the demands and delights of life. Goodness, then, is not a final or definitive resolution of some conflict, not obtaining or honoring a natural order, but rather an aesthetic of seeing and responding to conflict, chaos, and ambiguity. According to Karen McCarthy Brown, then, the authority of Alourdes "rests at least in part on the fact that she has an aesthetic sense rooted, not in the mere tolerance of clash and conflict, but rather in the positive enjoyment of it. She enjoys, and is accomplished at, the organization of power, of life energy.... In addition to her pleasure in giving form to energy, her aesthetic skill derives from a consummate sense of relationships and how these may be clarified and subtly changed to achieve a state that is at once dynamic and balanced."[62] Alourdes is valued not because she stands above, or "stands over and against her community," rather, she is valued because "she embodies it." What she embodies is a community, a "deeply-rooted traditional value system that accepts conflict, celebrates plurality, and seeks the good through whatever enhances life energy."[63]

Brown's discussion of moral responsiveness helps clarify the power of jazz. To see jazz as a moral catalyst does not require romanticizing jazz musicians as moral exemplars. Some of the artists venerated for their musical genius are also criticized for their insensitivity and abuse of others: "Bird was a most gifted innovator and evidently a most ingratiating and difficult man—one whose friends had no need for an enemy, and whose enemies had no difficulty in justifying their hate."[64]

There are, however, other jazz artists who have avoided the traps of self-indulgence and self-destruction and perform music characterized by depth, skill, and the insight born of many years of experience. Peter Watrous notes this dimension of the fruits of age. In a cutting contest in April 1996, "the saxophonists, Von Freeman, Teddy Edwards, Johnny Griffin and Joe Lovano (the first three hovering around their seventh decade), played with so much information and wit that the audience was left in awe of the music and not the physicality of the performance."[65]

Whatever the moral failings or strengths of the individual artists (shades of the Donatist Controversy), the music remains a catalytic force for creativity, resilience, and joy.[66] Hence the power of Mary

Lou Williams's admonition to inattentive audiences: "Listen, this will heal you."[67]

If we are grounded in a "value system that accepts conflict, celebrates plurality, and seeks the good through whatever enhances life energy,"[68] what do we have to offer those seeking meaning and direction? What comfort, what hope can be found within our nondualistic images of good and evil, our nondualistic understandings of power, moral agency, and social action? How about a postmodern answer to Kant's three questions: What can I know? What may I hope? What must I do?[69]

What can we know? We know more and more and are able to trust it less and less. We are inundated by knowledge about the world in which we live, aware of the historical and political matrix of our identities, learning more about human differences, and all the while aware that our knowledge of these "facts" about the world are themselves based on changing methods of discerning and creating the "true." What we know, while vast, rests on shaky foundations. Furthermore, as we attempt to ascertain the effects of our actions, we are challenged to keep in mind the law of unintended consequences: our actions, no mater how carefully thought out, have unpredictable ramifications, multiple consequences for good or ill—often, for both.

What may we hope? We may hope for resilience and company. We have hope for endurance, for companionship, for being able to respect and celebrate life in the company of friends and colleagues. We may also hope for a matrix for responding to challenges, not a means of resolving them once and for all. Finally, what must we do? Here the postmodern ethos is clear, offering an image of power and chaos, of vitality and humor, as we learn to live fully and act creatively in the midst of a world we can never control and can only partially understand.

3

"LEARNING TO SEE SIMULTANEOUSLY
YET DIFFERENTLY"

—Patricia Williams*

THE CHALLENGE OF MULTICULTURAL EDUCATION

I. CONNECTION

How do we maintain connection as a nation? What types of social relationships are necessary for justice, equality, and democracy? And what is the role of education in establishing those connections and those relationships? You'll notice I said connection, and not commonality; that I emphasized relationships, and not common ground. There is a debate in the United States over what it takes to maintain community. Does it require common ground, shared values, shared language, culture, and ideals? What is the place of difference within community—different histories, values, cultures, languages, experiences of access and/or discrimination? Can we affirm membership in a community and still be critical of key aspects of that community's values, practices, and history?

---

*Patricia Williams, *The Alchemy of Race and Rights: Diary of a Law Professor* (Cambridge, MA: Harvard University Press, 1991), p. 173.

Many people hold a dualistic notion of what it takes to maintain community. They argue that community is based on shared values and an unequivocal affirmation of cultural identity. Former Senator Bob Dole, for example, in his 1996 presidential campaign, gave a clear articulation of this dualistic understanding of identity and community. He criticized teachers and "elitist liberals" who are involved in a "shocking campaign" to "untie the string of citizenship." What does Dole see as "untying the strings"? First, under their tutelage "what was once good in the United States has become bad." Dole raises the fundamental issues at stake in multicultural education and in our understandings of democracy: "What we see as opportunity, they see as oppression.... Where we see a proud past, they see a legacy of shame. What we hold as moral truth, they call intolerance."[1]

What does it mean to acknowledge and affirm being American? For many of us, that identity is mixed, a complicated legacy of intolerance and openness, of exploitation and resistance, of opportunity and oppression. Dole rejects that ambiguity and proposes a profoundly dualistic view of community. In his world view it is either all or nothing: either opportunity or oppression, pride or shame, universal moral truth or intolerance. Dole adds another significant dimension to this dualistic world view: to value one's culture means that it has to be not just primarily good, but also supremely good. He criticizes those who "glorify other cultures" and claims that criticism of America and Western culture means disparaging America and the ideas and traditions of the West.[2] Dole also speaks of an "original concept of what it means to be an American" and claims that fidelity to this concept requires leaving diversity behind for sameness: "Our diversity requires us to bind ourselves to the American Idea in every way we can—by speaking one language, taking pride in our true history and embracing the traditional American values that have guided us from the beginning."[3]

Note all the claims of unambiguous truth: identity and values that have always been practiced, one set of values, one language. To challenge these assumptions, arguing that this "true" American history is not factual, is not the best in the world, and is not absolutely good, is seen as intrinsically destructive of community identity and unity. This concern is not limited to former Senator Bob Dole. Glenn C. Loury, for example, writes of "the absence of a sense of shared purpose transcending racial and ethnic boundaries—what Arthur Schlesinger, Jr. called 'the disuniting of America.'"[4]

Let's grant that there is a "disuniting" of America. We do interpret our history differently depending on who we are. Some see a history of opportunity; others see a history of opportunity for some and exploitation and limitation for many others. There are mutually incompatible views of the degrees to which American ideals of justice, freedom, and equality have been attained.[5] Furthermore, there are fundamental differences in theories of community: some who claim community requires sameness and is threatened by diversity, others who see community as being strengthened by diversity, enlivened by a blend of similarities and differences.

How much difference can a community hold? How much critique? These questions are not limited to members of the American majority. There are significant divisions among marginalized groups in the United States, divisions between women of all races, between people of color, between people who are working class or poor and yet are from different races. Take as an example divisions among Asian Americans in the United States. What is the connection between people who have immigrated to the United States from Korea, China, Vietnam, Japan, and Cambodia? These nations are hardly a united block. What is the carry-over to the United States of tensions between these nations? Furthermore, what is the relationship between people who have immigrated from Africa and Latin America with people who have been here for centuries—African Americans, Latinas/Latinos, and Native Americans, the original inhabitants of this land base. Is the only point of unity being not white, or not of European descent? Are the barriers to inclusion the same for each group?

How do we make sense of our multiple communities and our multiple identities? In her criticism of Adrienne Kennedy's plays, Margo Jefferson states the challenge clearly: "The real test of intelligence in America right now isn't just the ability to hold two opposing ideas in one's mind at the same time and still function, as F. Scott

Fitzgerald said: it's the ability to hold at least two opposing identities there as well."[6]

Who are we as Americans? Whose stories matter? Whose achievements and failures shape our sense of who we are and who we can be? At the core of multicultural education is a wager: a vital national identity can be constituted through multiplicity, ambiguity, and contradiction. Multicultural education shows us the reasons for a nondualistic understanding of community; it educates us about the history and culture that demonstrate the checkered past of America, the mixture of opportunity and exclusion, of freedom, and of institutionalized racism and sexism. Multicultural education also provides the analytical and emotional tools for living within a nondualistic understanding of self, group, and national identity. Healthy identity can include seeing failures and successes, acts of cruelty and compassion.

An honest look at the multiplicity of identity, history, and stories can also be seen in other dimensions of American culture. Ralph Ellison, for example, sees this sensibility, this identity fueled by ambiguity and contradiction, in the blues:

> The blues is an art of ambiguity, an assertion of the irrepressibly human over all circumstance whether created by others or by one's own human failings. They are the only consistent art in the United States which constantly remind us of our limitations while encouraging us to see how far we can actually go.[7]

"To remind us of our limitations while encouraging us to see how far we can actually go"—this is the challenge not just of the blues but also of multicultural education. We can live out the ideals of American democracy only if we forthrightly admit, study, and analyze the failures to implement those ideals.

What can be learned from the centuries-long campaign to end slavery and grant citizenship to all African Americans? What can be learned from ongoing struggles to have women seen as citizens—having the right to vote and equal protection under the law?

How do we account for the disparity between Enlightenment ideals of reason, justice, and equality and the practices of denying fundamental rights to women of all races, to people of color, to people of all races who are poor or working class? Patricia Williams writes of the complex process entailed in giving life to aspirations for justice and equal rights. Williams argues that equal rights have not been fairly extended to women and people of color. She cites as evidence the Tuskegee syphilis experiment carried out from 1932 until 1972, in which doctors within the U.S. public health service withheld treatment for syphilis from black men. Approximately 600 men died.[8] Williams claims that this experiment's failure was not one of theory but one of practice: "This country's worst historical moments have not been attributable to rights *assertion* but to a failure of rights commitment."[9]

Her criticism of the failures of rights commitment, the times when we have not lived up to our ideals of equality and justice, does not lead her to declare that those ideals are merely a sham, a hypocritical mask for exploitation and injustice. She tells a more complicated story—and not one simply of shame at not living up to our ideals of justice. Williams writes of the centuries-long process of giving practical form to cherished ideals:

> To say that blacks never fully believed in rights is true. Yet it is also true that blacks believed in them so much and so hard that we gave them life where there was none before.... This was the resurrection of life from ashes four hundred years old. The making of something out of nothing took immense alchemical fire—the fusion of a whole nation and the kindling of several generations.... But if it took this long to breathe life into a form whose shape had already been forged by society, and which is therefore idealistically if not ideologically accessible, imagine how long the struggle would be without even that sense of definition, without the power of that familiar vision.[10]

Does Williams's story mean that the values of the West are disparaged? By pointing to oppression and not opportunity, is there only shame? No. Williams's story of the African American centuries-long struggle to implement rights is a story of rage and pride. We find in Williams's analysis a story that leads us to a deeper understanding of the power of rights language; one enriched, not invalidated, by critiques of the failures to implement those rights; a story that challenges us to keep alive the alchemical fire that allows us to "give to all of society's objects and untouchables the rights of privacy, integrity, and self-assertion; give them distance and respect."[11]

> In discarding rights language altogether, one discards a symbol too deeply enmeshed in the psyche of the oppressed to lose without trauma and much resistance. Instead, society must *give* them away. Unlock them from reification by giving them to slaves. Give them to trees. Give them to cows. Give them to history. Give them to rivers and rocks. . . . Flood them with the animating spirit that rights mythology fires in this country's most oppressed psyches, and wash away the shrouds of inanimate-object status, so that we may say not that we own gold but that a luminous golden spirit owns us.[12]

What can we learn from the history of rights assertion and rights denial? We can see this history as a story of discovery, a story of learning to see people and peoples as worthy of privacy, integrity, self-assertion, distance, and respect.

I describe here *a* model of multicultural education as *one* component of learning from this story. Multicultural education is a "way to discover," a form of learning embued with an ethos that is nondualistic—intrinsically open-ended, contradictory, and yet vital and full of joy. It is a learning like that described by Muriel Rukeyser:

> Acknowledging opened water, possibility:
> open like a woman to this meaning.
> In a time of building statues of the stars,
> valuing certain partial ferocious skills
> while past us the chill and immense wilderness
> spreads its one-color wings until we know
> rock, water, flame, cloud, or the floor of the sea,
> the world is a sign, a way of speaking. To find.
> What shall we find? Energies, rhythms, journey.
>
> Ways to discover. The Song of the Way In.[13]

What is "the song of the way in"? Rather than bemoaning the disuniting of America, what do we do with these contradictory stories and values?

For many on the Left, the bottom has dropped out. There are deep-seated divisions among feminists, divisions between people concerned primarily with class and others who focus on race or gender. The manifold divisions within the progressive movement can be frightening, discouraging, and frustrating: in-fighting over who is most oppressed, or struggles over which issues should be addressed first. Audre Lorde describes the pain of these divisions within our groups, groups formerly seen as like us and providing a safe haven from a hostile world:

> Once when I walked into a room
> my eyes would seek out the one or two black faces
> for contact or reassurance or a sign
> I was not alone
> now walking into rooms full of black faces
> that would destroy me for any difference
> where shall my eyes look?
> Once it was easy to know
> who were my people.[14]

The divisions within progressive politics are exacerbated by the rejection of socialism in Eastern Europe and the loss of a unifying and compelling political vision. Nancy Fraser describes this as the postsocialist condition and claims it is has three constitutive features:

> The first is the absence of any credible progressive vision of an alternative to the present order. This, of course, is partly a matter of the increased delegitimation, in the wake of 1989, of socialism in the broad sense. What has collapsed, in other words, is not just a set of (erstwhile) actually existing institutional arrangements but belief in the principal ideal that inspired struggles for social transformation for the last century and a half. The immediate consequence is what Jürgen Habermas has called "the exhaustion of (leftwing) utopian energies." . . .
>
> The second constitutive feature of the "postsocialist" condition concerns a shift in the grammar of political claims-making. Claims for the recognition of group difference have become intensely salient in the recent period, at times eclipsing claims for social equality. . . .

The context for these developments, and the third defining fea-
ture of the "postsocialist" condition, is a resurgent economic liberalism. As the center of political gravity seems to shift from
redistribution to recognition, and egalitarian commitments
appear to recede, a globalizing wall-to-wall capitalism is
increasingly marketizing social relations, eroding social protec-
tions, and worsening the life-chances of billions.[15]

Fraser points to basic tensions within progressive politics. On the
one hand, we have a politics of recognition: "culturally defined
'groups' or 'communities of value' who are struggling to defend their
'identities,' end 'cultural domination,' and win 'recognition'."[16] On the
other hand, much of our theoretical work is based on a politics of
redistribution: "economically defined 'classes' struggling to defend
their 'interests,' end 'exploitation,' and win 'redistribution'."[17]

Using Fraser's terms, I see the problem as follows: claims of recognition are couched in the logic of affirmation and innocence, proposals
for redistribution are framed in the logic of utopia and stasis. That is,
we claim recognition as a group because we are the vanguard, the marginalized, the bearers of political insight and cultural integrity. Our
proposals for redistribution are valid because they solve problems of
injustice, they redress significant measures of political and economic
inequity. What happens, however, when we factor in undecidability,
ambiguity, and fault into each set of claims? The vanguard, the marginalized, are also complicitous in various forms of exclusion and
shaped by limitations; our attempts at redistribution, while effective
for a time, do not resolve all problems, do not remain in place (e.g., we
are, once again, having to stop child labor) and may themselves cause
other problems.[18]

I am offering a way of combining recognition and redistribution
without utopian visions or claims to innocence and virtue. This postsocialist era is also a time of growth, a time to see more clearly, to learn,
and to explore new options. I have no social theory to offer, no grand
political strategy but, rather, a process to offer, a way to be in the disuniting—I see multicultural education as a way to work with and
learn from conflicts, limits, and possibilities.

There is an alternative to the "political imaginary" of socialism, an alternative to the "political imaginary" of capitalism, an alternative to the "political imaginary" of any utopian dreams of unending progress, absolute justice, and beneficent power and creativity: rage and compassion in the face of suffering and injustice; resilience in the face of opposition and set-backs; laughter in the face of failure and mistakes; and virtuosity—audacious, breathtaking, disciplined, and heartfelt—in the face of limits.

II. "SEEING SIMULTANEOUSLY YET DIFFERENTLY" (PATRICIA WILLIAMS)

The disuniting of America has two strands: ambiguity and difference. The ambiguity emerges from a recognition of the injustices within American society; the place of difference emerges as an issue when we see the American story as the story of all the peoples of America with all of our differences of race, religion, class, sexual orientation, gender, and ethnicity. In order to understand these two strands and in order to live with them, we need a sense of self and community fluid enough to learn from and with difference and mistakes. What bothers me about the calls for common ground is that this very concept of community is predicated on denying what I see as the richness of community, a richness created as much by difference and surprise as by similarity and affirmation.

The emphasis on commonalties and common ground presumes a truncated vision of human relationships. The connections that give life meaning—that bring delight and joy, that evoke and sustain work to heal, to end injustice, to establish fairness—at times take the form of the shock of recognition. But just as often, the connections that give life meaning come from the shock of difference, of being surprised by the novelty of someone else's insight, by the jolt of unpredictability, by having someone act in a way that offers a different perspective, an unpredictable and telling social critique or alternative strategy for acting justly. A major aspect of the feeling of respect and of love is the joy of otherness—knowing that the other person or group exceeds our comprehension, prediction, and control. It is possible to respect, even to take pleasure in that which is outside our control, either conceptually or politically. In all of our interactions, there can be the place of familiarity and also openness to being surprised, to being challenged by the differences of another's way of seeing and acting.

Much of the experience of feeling love, even for those most familiar, is the juxtaposition of novelty and sameness, of difference and similarity; the jolt of seeing them, no matter how familiar, as utterly different, separate, their thoughts and feelings somehow unpredictable and unfathomable.

This is not to say that similarity is not comforting and is not essential. It is. What I am saying is that it is the blend of similarity and difference that enriches life—and that dualistic understandings of the self, of identity, of value, lead us to overemphasize similarity and miss what can be gained through difference.

Patricia Williams captures the jolt of otherness in her account of debates with her sister over the exact color of overheated highways:

> One summer when I was about six, my family drove to Maine. The highway was straight and hot and shimmered darkly in the sun. My sister and I sat in the back seat of the Studebaker and argued about what color the road was. I said black, she said purple. After I had harangued her into admitting that it was indeed black, my father gently pointed out that my sister still saw it as purple. I was unimpressed with the relevance of that at the time; but with the passage of years, and much more observation, I have come to see endless overheated highways as slightly more purple than black. My sister and I will probably argue about the hue of life's roads forever. But the lesson I learned from listening to her wild perceptions is that it really is possible to see things— even the most concrete things—simultaneously yet differently; and that seeing simultaneously yet differently is more easily done by two people than one, but that one person can get the hang of it with time and effort.[19]

How do we learn to see "simultaneously yet differently"? The ability to see and value difference is often misunderstood by those who focus on foundations of common ground, shared ideals, and same values. The ability to see simultaneously yet differently is better served by an acknowledgment of the relativism of our understandings of truth, justice, and beauty. Multicultural education helps us understand difference: it is the epistemology and pedagogy of politically engaged and politically accountable relativism.

What does relativism mean? Relativism is often misinterpreted by its critics as a lack of standards, grounds, and criteria. It is erroneously thought of as the twofold claim that there are no universal values and that there are no reasons for preferring one religion, one set of values, or one political system to another. To those who ground their claims about values and social structures in absolutes, in the truth about human nature, as discovered by science and/or history or as revealed by god or gods, to them, relativism seems to be saying anything goes. And yet nothing could be further from the truth. Within relativism, there are grounds for our claims about values and social structures: connections and relationships. The meaning of a system is determined by its relations—how is it related to the past, to possibilities in the present, and possibilities for whom and at what cost?[20]

Multicultural education does not mean the triumph of subjectivity. Rather, it is a process of learning to see the world through multiple lenses. What prevents complacency, and self-deluding certainty, under conditions of well-being? Difference. We need the vision and expertise of others to see where our views are partial and/or just plain wrong—inadequate in our understanding of the depth of oppression, inadequate in our strategies for establishing justice.

Many argue that we can only criticize current conditions as unjust because of our vision of an ideal world—a world of fairness, openness, and equality. I argue, however, that we can see the injustice in our system only when we are shaped by, or are in contact with, another system, one that demonstrates other possibilities of human sociality and respect. The source of critique is not an ideal but different realities, different dimensions of our own lives, and seeing different possibilities in the lives of others. Let me give a few examples: Aristotle and slavery, white Christians and racism, progressive critiques of American militarism.

Alasdair McIntyre claims that Aristotle's acceptance of slavery is accidental, not a fair measure of the adequacy of his ethical system.

While he argues that Aristotle's justification of slavery is "indefensible," he claims that it is unrelated to the adequacy of his ethics, that it "need not carry any large implications for our attitudes to his overall theory."[21]

What led to Aristotle's defense of slavery is, however, what is most dangerous in our own society: the assumption that one's own community and social class possess the prerequisites for moral judgment and that other groups are devoid of those same prerequisites. As McIntyre states, Aristotle dismisses non-Greeks, barbarians, and slaves as "incapable" of political relationships and thus incapable of participating in political forms that are necessary for the existence of virtue.[22] "He [Aristotle] seeks to be the rational voice of the best citizens of the best city-state; for he holds that the city-state is the *unique political form in which alone the virtues of human life can be genuinely and fully exhausted.*"[23]

The confidence in the superiority of the Aristotelian polis precludes being challenged by either the political systems and ethical standards of other communities or by the ethical standards and experiences of other groups (e.g., women and slaves) within the same community. What does it take to see forms of oppression that are taken for granted, that have existed for centuries and constitute integral parts of our way of life? We can avoid the dangers of isolation and self-justifying ethical systems by our involvement in political coalitions and by our openness to political conflict. Foundational ethical critique requires difference. Michel Foucault has argued that we can see a system of logic as partial and not as reason itself only because we participate in alternative systems of making and validating truth claims.[24] The same is true of ethics. We can see foundational flaws in systems of ethics only from the outside, from the perspective of another system of defining and implementing that which is valued. In order to determine which interests or positions are more just, pluralism is required—not for its own sake, but for the sake of enlarging our moral vision.[25]

To see these flaws, the ways our ideals are contradicted and invalidated by daily practices, by institutions and by culture, requires difference—requires listening to the experiences of others.

Lillian Smith's analysis of racism in the American South gives a poignant illustration of this dilemma. Smith wrote in the 1940s about a world of severe exploitation: not just economic discrimination, not just segregation (this is the Jim Crow era of separate schools, rest rooms, denial of access of blacks to restaurants, hotels, movie theaters), but also violence—the lynching of black men by whites and the rape of black women by white men. All of this violence constituted the texture of daily life and was masked by the surface politeness and courtesy of some whites toward blacks, masked by ideologies of Christian character and democratic ideals.

> Even its children knew that the South was in trouble . . . all knew that under quiet words and warmth and laughter, under the slow ease and tender concern about small matters, there was a heavy burden on all of us and as heavy a refusal to confess it. The children knew this "trouble" was bigger than they, bigger than their family, bigger than their church, so big that people turned away from its size. They had seen it flash out and shatter a town's peace, had felt it tear up all they believed in. They had measured its giant strength and felt weak when they remembered. . . . We knew guilt without understanding it, and there is no tie that binds men closer to the past and each other than that.[26]

Smith writes of being a child in the South, of learning the mutually incompatible virtues of Christian "brotherhood" and white supremacy:

> The mother who taught me what I know of tenderness and love and compassion taught me also the bleak rituals of keeping Negroes in their "place." The father who rebuked me for an air of superiority toward schoolmates from the mill and rounded out his rebuke by gravely reminding me that "all men are brothers," trained me in the steel-rigid decorums I must demand of every colored male. They who so gravely taught me to split my body from my mind and both from my "soul," taught me also to split my conscience from my acts and Christianity from southern tradition.[27]

What does it take to see internal contradictions in a society and its values? Difference. Lillian Smith writes as a white and to other whites, but also as one who has seen American society from the point of view of black Americans. She writes of an understanding of the present and of history that is lost to whites, trapped in self-deluding enclaves—not seeing the human beings they alternately romanticize, trivialize, and oppress.

> I knew that my old nurse who had cared for me through long months of illness, who had given me refuge when a little sister took my place as the baby of the family, who soothed, fed me, delighted me with her stories and games, let me fall asleep on her deep warm breast, was not worthy of the passionate love I felt for her but must be given instead a half-smiled-at affection similar to that which one feels for one's dog. I knew but I never believed it, that the deep respect I felt for her, the tenderness, the love, was a childish thing which every normal child outgrows.... I learned to use a soft voice to oil my words of superiority. I learned to cheapen with tears and sentimental talk of "my old mammy" one of the profound relationships of my life. I learned the bitterest thing a child can learn: that the human relations I valued most were held cheap by the world I lived in.[28]

What is the ground of Lillian Smith's critique? An ideal world of racial equality? No, fragmentary experiences of racial equality, moments of respect and interaction that then serve as the basis for social critique and transformation.

> From 1925 through 1948, Lillian Smith was the director of Laurel Falls Camp. There she provided for other young southern women the experiences that enabled them to see and challenge racism. There she began systematically to examine and then confront her society's concepts of race and gender. There also she came close to creating the world she wanted to live in, a world where every child could experience esteem, where individual creativity could be encouraged by a supportive community, where old ideas were questioned and new ones explored, and where differences could be appreciated. Encouraging emotional and psychological as well as physical development, Smith helped the daughters of white upper-class southerners question the world they lived in and begin to envision the possibility of change in that world.[29]

What maintains delusions of certainty and group superiority? Insularity. What enables foundational critiques of one's own society, and not just other peoples' oppressive behaviors and institutions? Difference. Richard Barnet highlights the significance of difference in his study of American militarism, *The Roots of War*.[30] A key component in being able to wage war on a people, a key component to confidently pursuing U.S. interests, uncomplicated by understanding the divergent interests of other nations, is distance. He writes of the policy of the state department of rotating people every two years. Without deep contact, there can be no engagement with difference and thus no foundational critique. If you do not know a people or culture well, you have no opportunity of seeing how their vision of their nation's well-being, or of global well-being, differs from that of the United States. Also, even if the ideal visions are shared, there is no opportunity to see if the policies chosen by the United States to implement those ideals actually work in that situation.[31]

> Robert McNamara was, of course, the leading specimen of *homo mathematicus*—i.e., men who behave and believe other men behave primarily in response to "hard data," usually numbers (infiltration rates, "kill ratios," bomb tonnage). Like the classic private eye on television, they are always looking for "the facts," but usually the wrong ones. They miss reality, for they never get close enough or related enough to another society to do more than count things in it. If you relate to a country as a military target you do not need to know anything about it except such details as are easily supplied by reconnaissance satellites. . . . You need never know who the victims of your attack were. . . . Things that stay still long enough to be counted are either inanimate or dead. Living human beings, complex and changing political relationships, intangibles like national pride elude the best analysis.[32]

What forms of community prevent reifying our own structures of oppression? The community that provides both home and critique, comfort and challenge, is one shaped by contiguity and similarity.

Joseph Maxwell writes of the seeming contradiction between community and diversity: "Educational, social, and political theory have generally assumed that diversity, despite its moral and practical benefits, is necessarily in tension with solidarity and community—that individual or group differences are intrinsically a source of conflict, and need to be overcome or transcended through the recognition or creation of commonalties."[33]

Maxwell cites definitions of multicultural education that operate from the assumption that "this goal of diversity within unity is inherently in tension with itself and will always generate disagreements about how much cultural difference is compatible with common political values, and how common the core must be."[34] Some advocates of multicultural education, and some social theorists, assume that solidarity is based on similarity. Maxwell cites Rorty's definitions; "Feelings of solidarity are necessarily a matter of which similarities and differences strike us as salient. . . . [Solidarity] is thought of as the ability to see more and more traditional differences (of tribe, religion, race, customs, and the like) as unimportant when compared to similarities."[35]

Maxwell points to an impasse in multicultural education—a respect for diversity, yet diversity is seen as a threat to solidarity. He offers a way out: solidarity can be based on both similarity and contiguity. That is, group identity can be bolstered by engagement with difference as much as by similarities.

> I argue that in all human societies, there are two fundamentally different dimensions of relationship that are involved in the creation and maintenance of solidarity: similarity and contiguity. Similarity-based solidarity derives from the ways in which people recognize or construct *resemblances* between one another, ways in which they are *alike*. Contiguity-based solidarity, on the other hand, derives from the ways in which people *interact,* meet one another's needs, and thereby come to know and care about one another. It is not inherently a matter of either similarity or difference; it is a separate dimension of relationship, often involving difference and compatibility rather than similarity. (The widespread characterization of community as involving both "common ties" and "social interaction" implicitly recognizes this distinction.) Contiguity is not limited to face-to-face

contact, though this is the paradigmatic case; it can involve relationships of interaction at a distance.[36]

While some tend to think of stable societies in terms of a shared
culture, "shared goals, motives, or beliefs," Maxwell reminds us that
anthropologists paint a more complex picture. Social cohesion can also
arise from the recognition and organization of diversity. There is room
for substantial heterogeneity within cultural groups.[37]

Maxwell describes cultures in which differences do not disrupt ties
of mutual caring and support. He cites Clifford Geertz's analysis of
traditional Javanese villages, where there is considerable solidarity
despite the fact that people have widely divergent religious beliefs.
What held people together? All participated in a common meal—the
slametan; "These villages exhibited a diverse range of belief systems,
including Hindu-based, Islamic and pancretistic elements, but individual differences in religious views were softened by the easy tolerance of the Javanese for a wide range of religious concepts, so long as
basic ritual patterns—that is, slametans—were supported."[38]

Maxwell also gives as an example his study of kinship in an Inuit
community; he found that relatives were defined by proximity, cooperation, and assistance, and not by biological ties.

> These Inuit have a "social metaphysic" that gives primacy to
> locality and participation as the basis for social connection, and
> that is central to the meaning of kinship, which is the main form
> of relationship in these communities. The term for relative, *ila,*
> has as its most general meaning "part" or "piece." In this broad-
> er sense, it is most commonly used, not for a part of homoge-
> neous mass, but for something which has a distinct identity yet is
> a necessary or functioning part of a larger whole, such as a part
> of a harpoon or motor. When used to refer to persons, *ila* means
> "partner" or "companion," as well as having the more specific
> meaning of "relative." These Inuit often do not acknowledge as
> relatives persons to whom they are biologically related but with
> whom they have had no interaction. They emphasize not just
> the physical proximity, but the cooperation and assistance
> between relatives, often giving as examples situations in which

one person is more capable than another, and thus able to help the other.[39]

Maxwell applies the theory of contiguity-based solidarity to social policy and to the goals of education. Many people have assumed that solidarity based on contiguity is a relic of premodern societies. Even if we would like to have communities based on contiguity, on face-to-face contact, it seems impossible in our mobile, industrialized world. In the modern world solidarity is based on similarity—a shared sense of national identity, beliefs, and motives.[40]

Maxwell goes on to state that each form of solidarity has its moral and political risks. When a community defines solidarity in terms of shared goals, beliefs, and attitudes, there is the danger of a rigid identity closed to critique and transformation. There are also dangers for communities based on contiguity: respect and accountability can be limited to people whom one knows, limited to locale and not encompassing people at a distance; honoring difference can also lead to the justification of hierarchy and exploitation—claiming, for example, that women are fundamentally different from men, our value determined by our relationship to men as wives, mothers, daughters, lovers, and assistants.[41]

The challenge of multicultural education is to build a sense of community based on contiguity. Within this type of community, similarities and differences are equally valued. Furthermore, the moral and political risks of insularity are explicitly addressed by deliberately expanding the reach of our connection to other people: working with, learning from, a wide range of people; and learning, thereby, not that we are all basically alike but that our differences are as valuable as our similarities.

Otherness can be exhilarating—the risk of waiting for someone else to respond, being ready to learn from that response about a person's character, about possible ways of acting politically. In her novel about a midwestern university, *Moo,* Jane Smiley describes this dual joy—trusting in some degree of similarity yet being prepared to be surprised by the response of others.

There was a juncture in every enterprise that Mrs. Walker savored. It was that moment when the success or failure of her plan seemed to move out of her control into the much more tenuous grip of someone else.... For some duration of time, her plan teetered upon the commitment, the competence, or the honesty of another person. This moment, these moments, always exhilarated her, and not only because, most of the time, she had judged correctly, asserted herself tactfully, and would know success. Another sort of exhilaration ... came from the risk itself.[42]

What makes the risk exhilarating rather than terrifying? Exhilaration comes from the play of similarity and difference, familiarity and surprise. Communities based on contiguity can have the energy and creativity of jazz; community identity and structure can be improvisational, a fitting response to the needs of the moment and the strengths and resources of this people, at this place, and at this time. Our communities can be grounded in a set of "chord progressions," communal meals, festivals, cooperative work projects, and in a repertoire of responding to the wide range of human actions—cruelty and kindness, neglect and attention, cowardice and courage, greed and generosity.[43]

Multicultural education can be similar to playing jazz. Our teaching is not completely open-ended. It is open, but the openness, the space for new discoveries and insights, is deliberately evoked. We set in play structures—assigned readings, group activities, research and writing assignments—that establish the connections that allow us to be sparked by the insights and creativity of other students. It is not always easy, however, to get people to speak or to learn from each other. There are barriers, some due to oppression—women, for example, who because of sexism, are afraid of speaking, afraid that they will be ignored or ridiculed. Others find it difficult to listen to people from a different race or social class.[44] The structure of the class functions like a chord progression, addressing these barriers and establishing connections between disparate groups. What happens, then, with those connections is essentially improvisational.[45] Sometimes insights are reached similar to those of other years, sometimes the insights are new. We do not privilege novelty per se. It is as rewarding when students grasp fully for themselves the possibilities of challenging racism as when they see patterns of oppression or possibilities of justice that others had not envisioned.

What then, are the goals of multicultural education? In multicultural education we try to answer a series of questions—simple in their phrasing, endlessly complex in their answers.

Who are we, as a nation, a people, a city, a state, an age, a race, a gender, a family, an ethnicity, a sexual orientation? Whose stories shape us? Where do we come from? How do we learn what is true and what is just? How do we learn from our mistakes? To whom are we accountable? And, what brings us the deepest joy?

The answers to these questions lie in our connections to our past, to people and nature in the present, to nature and people in the future. While some think we have lost a healthy connection to family, community, and nation, many others see things in a radically different light. We do not bemoan the loss of the traditional family, for it had its flaws: absent fathers, oppressed mothers, unnamed and unchallenged incest and sexual abuse.[46] We do not bemoan the loss of traditional community ties. We remember the idealized 1950s were the time of rampant racism and legalized racial segregation, of red-baiting and McCarthyism, a time when a clear sense of national identity fueled a costly and potentially devastating nuclear arms race.

We have lost certainty, but it was the certainty of a mask that hid even from ourselves the disparity between ideals and practices.

III. "WAYS TO DISCOVER ... THE SONG OF THE WAY IN" (RUKEYSER)

Multicultural education is one place where people are forging a collective identity in response to our multiple stories, our manifold problems, our various and variegated possibilities of living fairly and well. Sleeter and Grant have identified and analyzed five basic models of multicultural education.[47] Each model of multicultural education provides a different answer to three basic questions: How just is American society? What is the role of schooling in preparing students to be part of this society? And, what are the differences among children that need to be taken into account in this preparation?

Model I

Sleeter and Grant describe the five models of multicultural education as follows. The first model of multicultural education is teaching the exceptional and the culturally different. This model is favored by people who think that the American political system is basically sound. The goal of multicultural education is helping all students fit into a fundamentally equitable mainstream. In order to make this happen, teachers need to be aware of the differences that impede assimilation and adaptation.[48] Model two is the human relations approach. Here society is still seen as basically equitable. What is most needed, however, for successful integration are human relations skills—learning to respect cultural differences, learning to empathize with those who are different, overcoming prejudice, and learning how to communicate effectively across cultures.[49] With model three, the political orientation changes. Advocates of model three, single group studies (women's studies, black studies, other forms of ethnic studies, gay and lesbian studies) claim that American society is unjust in significant ways. The goal of education is not assimilation but transformation—changing the mainstream rather than helping people accommodate to it. The goal is raising consciousness about oppression and mobilizing people for action.[50] Model four is multicultural education: again, society is criticized as being deficient, a deficiency that is remedied if we learn to celebrate, and not just tolerate, racial, sexual, ethnic, and cultural diversity and provide equal opportunity for all.[51] The fifth model, education that is multicultural and social reconstructionist, begins with the conviction that American society is significantly unjust, and that the goal of multicultural education is not simply celebrating diversity but also recognizing and challenging the inequitable power relations between different groups.[52]

Let's look at Sleeter's and Grant's analysis of these models of education in more detail. The goal of model one, teaching the exceptional and the culturally different, is clear-cut: assimilation into the mainstream. The political analysis is that American society is basically just, and that if people are not successful, it is due to "lack of skills, values, or knowledge." People who advocate this model realize that there is social inequality, but they perceive the cause of this inequality to be a lack of proper education and socialization. Within this model, beginning with the same political analysis, there are two options. Some people feel the barriers to assimilation and equality are caused by deficiencies in certain groups of students; others see differences but not deficiencies as the barrier to inclusion. The deficiency model presupposes that groups that are not as successful as others—African Americans, girls, children who are poor or working class, student with disabilities—are lacking fundamental intellectual and social skills.[53]

There is another strand of education within model one that is sharply critical of this deficiency orientation. While sharing the basic political analysis, some educators argue that the analysis of deficiencies is fundamentally inaccurate. They claim that differences are construed only as weaknesses, and that the strengths of different cultural groups are not recognized. In this model, the goal is the same—assimilation— but the problem is deduced to be inappropriate teaching, teaching that fails to bridge cultural differences.[54]

In this framework, so-called disabilities also have strengths—thus deafness can be interpreted in terms of deaf culture and not just as deficiency. Mental differences, from below average to gifted, are interpreted in the same way. Within this view, gender emerges as a significant variable: given their different socialization, girls, for instance, need grounding in the kinds of games that facilitate mathematical reasoning.[55]

The goal here is not remediation, as in the deficiency model, but excellence for all students. Teachers focus on different learning styles and using students' own cultures as a basis for moving into a mainstream culture. Sleeter and Grant claim that there are elements of this model that are incorporated into all models of multicultural education: there are skills and concepts that all students can learn; it is important to teach code-switching; students do have different learning styles. They describe, however, two basic ideas/conclusions that lead people to reject model one. First off, many people have a different analysis of the causes of inequality. What does it take to be fully incorporated into American Society? The advocates of model two claim that emotional and interpersonal skills are needed as much as skills in English, abstract reasoning, and mathematics. Those who prefer models three, four, and five emphasize structural barriers to inclusion—racism, sexism, class inequality, and homophobia—that prevent some people from being fully assimilated into the American mainstream.[56]

Sleeter and Grant give a second reason for rejecting model one, a strong critique of the goal of assimilation. People who advocate models three, four, and five claim that multicultural education is about changing the mainstream—about learning from other cultures and building with them an inclusive national identity. Once we start down this line of thinking, the definition of the "basics" begins to blur. Yes, all children need to learn to read. But wouldn't our culture be stronger if we all learned to tell stories? Are there not skills of memorization, of drama, of deep understanding, conveyed by being part of an oral tradition? Are there habits of thinking, of observation, that are part of Native American traditions that could help non–Native American students? As for code-switching, while it is helpful to move from Black English to white, middle-class, urban English, what about the reverse? What can be conveyed in Black English that is lost, muted, or distorted in white English?[57]

We will return to those questions about basic academic skills and knowledge with models three, four, and five. With model two we focus on interpersonal skills and on "basic" values.

Model 2

Sleeter and Grant state that the human relations approach to multicultural education, model two, builds on the post–World War II intercultural education. Like those who advocate model one, most advocates of model two believe American society is fundamentally just. They believe that it is possible for all to be included in our democratic society. In addition to academic skills, however, advocates of this model focus on the interpersonal skills necessary for democracy. The goal of model two is to help students recognize the common humanity of all people. What does it take to establish such respect? An acknowledgment and appreciation of the differences between individuals, between groups, between cultures. Unlike model one, which focuses on the needs of the deficient or different "other," model two addresses all people, those part of the majority culture as well as those within smaller groups.[58]

What does it take to work effectively with individuals within one's own cultural group who are different in significant ways? What does it take to work effectively, to communicate clearly, with people from other cultures? According to Sleeter and Grant the answers include learning more about one's own social group, and developing the skills required for group work. A key task of human relations training is developing a strong sense of group identity and pride without demeaning others. That is, being good does not have to mean being better than or being best.[59] Learning this way of being in a group is as much a matter of emotional skill as learning information; and it is a psychological strength that is essential for democracy.

People who practice the human relations model believe that interpersonal and intergroup skills can and must be taught. In teaching these skills, they draw on theories of prejudice and bigotry, studies of the psychological components that impede working well with people and groups that are different. Although advocates of this model believe American society is fundamentally just, they see prejudice and bigotry as significant barriers to the full implementation of democracy.[60]

What are the strategies for challenging prejudice and bigotry? For prejudice, teachers focus on creating planned dissonance, exposing students to experiences, people, and information that demonstrate the inaccuracy of stereotypes. For bigotry, the focus is on creating a form of group identity that does not require scapegoating and hatred; to challenge bigotry it is essential to form groups in which pride does not entail being superior to other groups.[61]

Sleeter and Grant provide specific examples of how to challenge prejudice and bigotry. First, provide accurate information about individuals within one's own group who are different, and about other cultures. Human relations training includes much more, however, than providing accurate information. Educators spark cognitive dissonance by having students from different cultures work together on class projects. The project may have nothing to do with diversity or cultural awareness, but by pairing girls and boys, for example, to work in math or science projects, the teacher may break down stereotypes.[62]

A third strategy in the human relations model is to provide exercises and assignments that foster empathy between groups. Literature, role-playing, film, simulation games, all help student imagine what it is like to be someone else.[63]

A fourth type of activity used within model two is community action projects with people who are stereotyped by one's students. Working on community clean-up projects, or in community theater groups with people who are the objects of prejudice and bigotry, helps students see the fallacy of their prejudices. A fifth type of activity is directed toward stereotyping in the classroom, acknowledging when name calling or sexual harassment occurs, pointing out the negative effects of these behaviors, and involving the class in developing guidelines to prevent these behaviors.[64]

Sleeter and Grant state that model two is the most popular form of multicultural education for white elementary school teachers but, along with model one, the least favored by people who train in multicultural education. Why the disparity? Many people criticize model two not for what it does, but for what it does not do. Those who advocate model one claim that too much attention to model two detracts from academic achievement. For others, this approach merely addresses the symptoms of prejudice without examining why prejudices occur. They argue that the approach overlooks injustice and competition between groups. Furthermore, the focus is too individualistic, changing individual attitudes without critically examining the social stratification that creates those attitudes. Why are girls pictured as passive? Whose interests does that serve? Some claim that used alone, model two reinforces the status quo, reducing complex social problems to a simple matter of individuals treating each other with respect.[65]

Sleeter and Grant soften their initially harsh criticism. Even people who advocate models three, four, and five often state that model two is appropriate for young children, preschool through third grade. While it is appropriate to address issues of injustice as the children bring them to the class, kindergarteners are too young to be taught the full costs of oppression. Done well, the model serves as a foundation for other forms of multicultural education.[66]

What does it mean to do this model well? Sleeter and Grant argue that it requires acknowledging and valuing the commonalities and differences of the children in the classroom. Even racially homogenous classes are different in significant ways—social class, gender, religious traditions, learning styles, interests, relative abilities and disabilities. After acknowledging and valuing the commonalties and differences of the children in the classroom, children can learn about other cultures. Here it is important to avoid the "tourist" approach, focusing only on the exotic aspects of other cultures. All cultures are presented in as rich and detailed a manner as possible. Empathy requires seeing differences and similarities in daily routines such as schooling, family life, games, and music.[67]

Model 3

Sleeter and Grant find that the third model of multicultural education, single group studies, begins with a clear political analysis and goal. American society is unjust, and the implementation of democracy requires understanding and rectifying that injustice. Thus, all students need to learn more about the experiences and histories of marginalized groups. Furthermore, those students who belong to marginalized groups need to be empowered to participate fully in all aspects of American society. That participation is not adequately understood as assimilation, for the full inclusion of women, people of color, gays, and lesbians will reshape the American mainstream.[68]

Advocates of single group studies claim that American society is unjust and that the educational system has perpetuated that injustice. Education has not been neutral and has served the interests of the few. Single group studies seek to challenge that exclusivity; they widen the literary canon to include the work of women and people of color, they deepen and expand the history of American society to incorporate the history of all Americans.[69]

There is a vast amount to be learned about working-class Americans, about deaf culture, about women's history, about the culture and history of Native Americans, Asian Americans, African Americans, Hispanics, Chicanos, and Latinos/Latinas. There is an explosion of scholarship in all of these fields. We are looking at the experiences, stories, cultures and art of the vast majority of humankind for the first time.[70]

Sleeter and Grant highlight the political function of model three. Single group studies directly analyzes social inequality and promotes the equality of the group studied. Its aim is to empower groups by providing the information that serves as the basis for social action. This information is important for all students to learn, those from dominant as well as marginalized groups. The information is complex and nuanced and cannot be understood if addressed in a piecemeal fashion. The work is done from the point of view of the group being studied, examining in depth what is significant to that group. The next step is to examine differences within the group along with the intricacies of bias, discrimination, exclusion, exploitation, and oppression (e.g., Iris Marion Young's analysis of the five faces of oppression).[71] What function do bias and oppression serve for the dominant group? How is that bias and oppression justified, denied, or masked by the dominant culture? Another dimension, equally important, is the recognition that oppressed groups are not merely oppressed but are also survivors, also creative shapers of culture and society. Given that oppressed groups are more than the history of oppression, what have been their contributions to American culture? What are the advantages of their full participation in American society? How can they change the mainstream values and policies? And finally, what strategies have been effective or ineffective in bringing about transformation and inclusion?[72]

Model 4

Model four, what Sleeter and Grant call multicultural education, is a synthesis of model two and the scholarship produced by single group studies. The goal of model four is to promote an understanding of and respect for all groups that make up American society, to help all children succeed academically, to teach all students about past and current inequities in American society. Advocates of this approach utilize multiple perspectives wherever possible. Multicultural education redefines literacy to include cultural literacy, helping white students learn about African American culture and history, for example, and their impact on African American as well as Euro-American culture.[73]

Model 5

Model five, education that is multicultural and social reconstructionist (the model preferred by Sleeter and Grant), adds a political component to model four. In addition to teaching about forms of social inequality, model five seeks to transform that inequality. This transformation occurs at three levels. First, education that is multicultural and social reconstructionist transforms the power relations within the school system. Second, educators examine the way the school reflects social inequality in staffing as well as in curriculum, and seek to remedy that inequality by changing hiring practices—hiring more women principals and superintendents, for instance, or insuring that the teachers and administrators reflect the racial and ethnic diversity of the community. What does it mean to practice democracy within the school? Advocates of model five focus on how the insights and concerns of teachers, staff, and families should be as influential as those of the school administrators and school board. It also promotes giving students as many choices as possible—practicing democracy in setting school rules or in working on group projects, for example.[74] Third, the political agenda of model five also extends beyond the classroom and the school system into the wider society. Part of education for democracy is practice in social action—not just analyzing injustice or social problems but also doing something about them—writing letters, participating in community service, educating others in the community about the problem.[75]

What do we have so far? The first two models of multicultural education begin with the premise that American society is basically just and focus on providing the skills necessary to participate in a democratic society—though they differ as to which skills are needed.

The first model, teaching the exceptional and the culturally different, assumes that most children have the requisite values and can readily develop the skills needed for academic and personal success, but that some children, because of cultural differences or disabilities, need special attention and help in assimilating into the mainstream. The second model, the human relations approach, also focuses on assimilation into a democratic society, but emphasizes skills in interpersonal and group relations. Advocates of this model argue that everyone, whatever their gender, race, or class, needs to be taught how to work within groups, how to overcome prejudice and bigotry, how to respect and value individual and cultural differences.

Although the remaining three models have, superficially, the same goal—that of preparing students to participate fully in a democratic society—they begin from a radically different political premise. Models three, four, and five point to how far we are from being a democratic society. They all acknowledge and seek to rectify the disparity between democratic ideals and social inequity, but they differ in how they address these needs. Model three, single group studies, focuses in depth on marginalized groups, aiming at empowering those groups; model four, multicultural education, observes reality from multiple perspectives; and model five, education that is multicultural and social reconstructionist, builds on the analytical work of models three and four, the human relations skill of model two, and adds an explicit social action agenda of bringing equity to the classroom and to the wider social environment.

What does it really take to fulfill the goals of model five? My work in model three, single group studies—specifically black studies and women's studies—has made it clear that the barriers to full equality are political, economic, cultural, and psychological. Recognizing that oppression and empowerment includes psychological and sociological factors leads me to a renewed emphasis on model two. We need model two in order to have the strength to see and rectify the injustices disclosed by models three through five.

From my work with models four and five, trying to integrate the lessons of women's studies, black studies, and an analysis of class, I have seen that single group studies are not only, by definition, partial, but also often shaped by dangerously romantic notions of group identity. For example, one cannot look at the experience and history of African Americans without noting sexism and homophobia within white and black communities, and the effects these forms of discrimination have had in shaping the complexities of African American history and life.[76] Similarly, to look at gender alone is not to see women fully. White women, even in our work for gender equality, are shaped as much by our race as by our society's definitions of womanhood.[77] Women's studies has been influenced by women of color providing compelling analyses of the interaction of race, gender, and class in our individual and collective identity; the same is beginning to be done by white women.[78] As we take seriously the complexities and ambiguities of our constructed and contested identities, something else emerges, suspicion about idealizing the "oppressed" and demonizing the "oppressors." Working with models four and five returns us to model three with greater depth and precision, seeing the ambiguity and complexity within marginalized groups, realizing that there is more to our errors, our abuses of power, our failures, than "internalized oppression."

In the remaining chapters I depict a self-conscious, critical, open-ended, nondualistic process of playing a very high-stakes game—shaping, defining, questioning, evaluating the very meanings of self, group, community, creativity, vitality, freedom, and responsibility. As I stated earlier, multicultural education shows us the reasons for nondualistic understandings of community by providing education about history and culture that demonstrates the checkered history of America, of the mixture of opportunity and exclusion, of freedom, and of institutionalized racism and sexism. Multicultural education also provides the analytical and emotional tools for living within a nondualistic understanding of self, group, and national identity.

4

"The Art of Ambiguity"

The blues is an art of ambiguity, an assertion of the irrepressibly
human over all circumstance whether created by others or by one's
own human failings. They are the only consistent art in the United
States which constantly remind us of our limitations while encouraging us to see how far we can actually go.   —Ralph Ellison

There are two common approaches to multicultural education
and diversity training that fall far short of the "art of ambiguity." One approach seeks to heighten conflict, and begins by
telling whites that they are racist and men that they are sexist. The
goal is to evoke change in dominant groups by forcing them to see
their own privilege and by confronting them with the rage of those
who are oppressed.

Another approach that falls short of the art of ambiguity is the
claim that this workshop, this class, is "safe space." One of the central
goals of much of the women's movement was the creation of "safe
space." The concept of "safe space" emerged from the consciousness-
raising movement; women, in small groups, telling each other the stories of our lives, and finding affinities, support, and insight. One basic
tool was asking questions of clarification. The rule was never to

criticize another woman but instead to ask, what did you mean by that, why do you say that, why do you think that? From these "safe" conversations, we learned that what we had experienced as personal suffering—feeling trapped in abusive relationships, not being hired or promoted—were not due to our own failures, were not just our private, individual misfortunes, but had a collective aspect. A key element of these gatherings was the experience, unique to many women, of being listened to with respect. As Nelle Morton describes it, "We heard ourselves into speech."[1] For many, it was the first time their insights and words were valued. Being silenced by men, afraid to speak, many women flourished in these settings, and discovered new insights about ourselves and our society.

While much good work was done in such settings, the expectations they set for the context of "real" conversation could not withstand the challenges of diversity. Safety was predicated on uniformity. Once difference arose (differences of race, class, and sexual orientation, different experiences of motherhood; differences that were not benign but constituted through unjust power relationships), the concept of safety, rather than eliciting speech, silenced it. There was no room for women to speak who wanted to challenge what was said, who wanted to point out how they were limited and controlled not just by men but also by women, and sometimes by the women in the room. Charges that other women were also oppressive were especially hard to hear.[2]

What do we do with these tensions? What does it mean to create an ethic of conflict, protocols for coalitions and conversations, where we can disagree without destroying each other? As bell hooks claims, sisterhood is a task, not a gift.[3] Building sisterhood requires learning how to live through conflict, learning how to elicit and learn from critique and disagreement. Rather than seeing serious disagreement as a sign of failure, it is possible to take disagreement as an invitation to a deeper relationship.

How do we understand differences? How do we play them? How do we learn from them about our capacity for harm, for complicity in injustice?

My work in multicultural education and diversity training represents a third model. We do not claim that the space here is "safe"; nor do we seek to humiliate people or elicit intense conflict. Instead, our goal is to learn how to grow from the process of open conflict and disagreement.

I bring five basic assumptions to my work in multicultural education. They are not, by any means, unique to me. The first, an affirmation of the importance and challenge of democracy, is also advocated by Peter McClaren, Henry Giroux, and Rebecca Chopp.[4] The other four I learned from diversity training workshops at the University of Missouri, workshops based on the model developed by the Equity Institute.[5] The assumptions are as follows:

1. Democracy is a goal that is both worthwhile and difficult to achieve.

2. Bias, exclusion, discrimination, exploitation, and oppression are pervasive and hurt everyone.

3. People and institutions do grow and change.

4. What motivates change is accountability, not guilt.

5. Establishing justice and practicing democracy is a lifelong process.

I. DEMOCRACY

Carol Lee Sanchez provides a compelling description of the longing for democracy and for equal rights:

> You are America and my father.
> your honesty
> your uncompromising faith in
> participatory democracy
> your belief in "the rights of the people"
> I take from you
> as my own—
> to pass on to future generations.[6]

What is necessary to practice these beliefs in democracy and equal rights? Both an affirmation of their value and a forthright acknowledgment of their failure to be implemented. It is this dual vision, this awareness of possibilities of justice and the actuality of injustice, that Patricia Williams sees as the constituent of "alchemical fire," the energy that makes real the possibilities for decency, equity, and transformation.

What is the alchemical fire that can transform the "familiar visions" of human equality into impassioned work for social justice? What is the alchemy that frees whites from the community-destroying distortions of racism? Do we need a reformation of our political ideals of democracy, human agency, human worth, and accountability? No. What we need is greater attention to practice, to the habits of living that can give us the courage and vision to live out the mandates of participatory democracy.

What is required for democracy? Commitment to an ideal, awareness of its failures, and practice. I am here relying on a very old tradition, the basic relationship between habits and virtue described by Aristotle.[7] We do not act virtuously by committing ourselves to grand ideals and saving our efforts for major, unambiguous challenges. Rather, we develop the virtue of courage, of justice, by acting regularly in small ways. Virtue has to be practiced, built up, cultivated. There is, then, a direct relationship between the choices of daily life and what choices we can make in the public sphere. If we cannot muster the strength or insight to address creatively racist or sexist remarks by friends and family, their personal habits of ignoring the rights of others, we cannot expect to have the courage and insight to respond creatively to structural problems: to the welfare policies that harm millions of children and deny basic human rights and dignity, to major events like the Holocaust, the brutal warfare in Bosnia and Rwanda.

The question, however, remains open of what counts as virtue. What Aristotle called virtue I see as vice. He extolled the practice of domination: domination within the self, of mind over body, of free-born, propertied males over wife, children, and slaves—all part of the practice of rule necessary for participation in governing the city-state.

The ethic of the Aristotelian polis was intrinsically one of exclusion, limited to the relationships of free men. In Michel Foucault's detailed description of the ethical categories through which classical Greek culture (fourth century B.C.E.) understood the use and limits of sexuality, I find a clear connection between what a particular society considered normative and the maintenance of oppression. Foucault states that the ethical systems developed by Plato and Aristotle were not meant to be universally applicable but were, quite self-consciously, an ethics for free men.[8] Within this ethical system, freedom did not mean independence "of any exterior or interior constraint; in its full positive form it was a power that one brought to bear on oneself in the power that one exercised over others."[9] Foucault states that "virtue was not conceived as a state of integrity, but as a relationship of domination, a relation of mastery."[10] For Aristotle and for Plato, "self-mastery and the mastery of others were regarded as having the same form; ... one was expected to govern oneself in the same manner as one governed one's household (women and slaves) and played one's role in the city."[11]

While I disagree with Aristotle's definition of virtue, I agree with his understanding of how the practice of virtue is inculcated through habits that affect individual actions; relationships with nature, family, and friends; group dynamics; relationships between groups, even between nations. Multicultural education, in its attention to habits of respect and risk-taking, then becomes the training ground for democracy. It is a training ground in three senses: (1) it teaches the vision, (2) it demonstrates where it is not implemented, and (3) it develops the habits of thinking, of analysis, of respecting and working with differences that constitute the practice of democracy.

In developing these habits, it is important to remember that democracy is not easily obtained. There are costs and benefits, pitfalls to be avoided, hard work to be done. It is difficult to embody democracy for two reasons: democracy is intrinsically conflictual, and the American affirmation of democracy is equivocal at best. There are other values, held with equal or greater force, that counter the practice of democracy: the desire for security, the certainty of being right in regard to important issues (e.g., abortion, death penalty, welfare, military policy, environmental responsibility, same-sex marriage), and wanting to silence permanently those who hold different views.

How do we develop the practice of respect so essential for a democratic society? The habit of respect is intrinsically rewarding, often difficult, and, at times, extremely tedious.

Democracy is not "natural." Learning from and with difference requires cultivation. Furthermore, the cultivation of respect is holistic, incorporating emotions, intellect, and even physical discipline. Multicultural education can be understood as a form of what Theophus Smith calls conjure: political, spiritual, and cultural transformation. For a culture to be transformed, mere policy changes are not enough. Moving from a culture based on dominance, moving from dualistic and apocalyptic forms of identity to living with the opportunities and conflicts of a pluralistic society, requires emotional and physical strength, requires resilience and imagination.

Ideas are not enough. Do our ideals fail because we do not know whether to believe in them? No. Our ideals fail because we do not know how to live them. And, this task of learning how to live them is both collective and individual, a task that requires art and analysis, reflection and praxis, laughter and rage.

Carol Lee Sanchez writes of "pass[ing] on to future generations" her father's belief in participatory democracy. What does it take to pass this belief on? What does it take to remember a lesson? To know it, hold to it, have it last for years, possibly generations? Freud, Nietzsche, Foucault, and Girard speak of lasting lessons being driven into the mind, body, and spirit through pain, sacrifice, and loss. I offer here an alternative: lessons, ways of seeing, of responding to the challenges of life, inculcated not through pain but through persistence, discipline, and joy. Persistence and discipline are crucial, the steady repetition of habits of listening, observing, waiting, and taking risks. Joy is also essential. Remember Charlie Parker and the sheer delight of virtuosity in the face of limits. This is a discipline of celebration and gratitude, gratitude for the joy of being in relationships to earth, sea, and sky, to animals, plants, and people. I am proposing a pedagogy of persistence, bull-headed endurance, and joy to counter the riveting, soul-searing pedagogy of pain and sacrifice. Does the pedagogy of pain and sacrifice work? Yes. Is it real? Yes. Is it part of human nature, of the "natural" human repertoire of responding to challenges and to fear? Most assuredly. Is it the only way of learning deeply, of establishing and maintaining social bonds? Most assuredly not!

In her poem, "the old ones" Carol Lee Sanchez describes "the message [she] needs to hear," a message from the old ones that challenges patterns of fragmentation and destruction.

> the old ones make patterns
> just outside my perception;
> external blueprints move to appear
> from beyond visibility.
> I cannot unfocus enough
> to refocus on the message
> I need to hear.
> my life crammed with:
>   bits of lives
>   scraps of ideals
>   pieces of change
> that belong to fragmented visions:
>   not on my own.
> it is the killing of things—that bothers.
> the separation of: this from that
> the analytical shattering of:
>   countless living things.[12]

In contrast to the "analytical shattering of living things," the old ones offer a point of focus and balance, habits I would say, of observation and respect.

> and they say:
> you must learn to observe everything
> so you will know and understand your own power
> the power of your own way.
> you should learn these things: carefully
> if you are not careful: you will hurt yourself

the old ones come
appear at the edges of my vision
remind me to care for myself—and
the *words* I discover
for:
(they say
words
are like singing.
words are like singing[13]

Being careful for oneself and the life we share, discovering the "words that are like singing," this is the gift, this the challenge of educating deeply and well.

II. CHANGE IS POSSIBLE

What makes us think that change is possible? From a postmodern understanding of democracy and of human nature, we can claim that change is possible but not inevitable. Some see all human beings as naturally endowed with reason and naturally able to respect each other, and, because of these essential attributes of human nature, able to participate in and flourish within democratic structures. I see democracy and the human nature and sociality that sustain democracy as a wager: one way of being human among many others, one way of being human that has to be nurtured and cultivated.

People are capable of vastly different forms of sociality: despotism, fascism, feudalism, democracy. Human nature is capable of domination and exclusion—wars of conquest and genocide. It is meaningless to separate nature and nurture, arguing that some tendencies are biological, others merely social. Thomas Berry in *Dreams of the Earth* juxtaposes natural human tendencies of respect for nature and each other with the cultural legacy of exploitation of the environment and other people.[14] What is the basis of the culture of exploitation if not a dimension of our nature? Better here to take the view of human nature true of some Native American peoples. As Carol Lee Sanchez states, the ground of Native American stories about ecological responsibility—ritual practices to express respect for all aspects of nature, for other human beings—is not a natural connection with the land but rather a memory of despoiling the land, of making choices that led to the depletion of wild life, and led to group conflict. Knowing that harmony can be lost, rituals and stories call people to habits of attention, ways of observing self and others, that can maintain harmony and balance.[15]

Our work for multicultural education is compelled by both realities: continuous injustice and people who resist that injustice. This is true even of seemingly intractable social problems. How do we curb, for example, the amount of crime perpetuated by young people? According to Peter Applebome, a "pool of 2,000 teenagers conducted by Louis Harris and Associates found that 1 in 8 youths—and almost 2 in 5 from high-crime neighborhoods—reported carrying a weapon for protection. One in 9, and more than 1 in 3 in high-crime neighborhoods, said they had cut class or stayed away from school at times because of their fear."[16] How do we counter this response—violence as the means of protection against violence? Do we appeal to an ideal world of nonviolence and cooperation? Do we posit a counterfactual but essential capacity for cooperation and empathy? No. We can foster the alternatives to violence that already exist, the alternative realities of empathy and nonviolence present even in those who have perpetuated violence. Applebome quotes the words of Suzanne Marrazzo, a teacher of juvenile offenders: "Nobody is better equipped to deal with it [violence] than the kids themselves. Even the most hardened ones can show amazing empathy when they talk about crime with younger kids. Their hearts are in the right place. But whether they would follow through and make a commitment, I'm not sure."[17]

What does it take to help people follow through on their good intentions? What does it take to establish justice? According to Stanley Crouch (and many others), it takes "universal humanism": "Our history, like the history of the world since the Enlightenment, is either one of adopting, expanding, and acting on the vision of universal humanity or rejecting it, since there can neither be thorough democracy nor a world morality based on the recognition of fundamental commonality without universal humanism."[18] What Crouch describes as a given, the foundation of social critique and political vision, I see as a task: an actuality embodied in the actions and attitudes of some people at particular times, and worthy of expansion, support, and ongoing self-critical development.

For example, how do we effectively challenge social structures that deny the full humanity of women? We see women as having full dignity with men. Yet, this simple conviction is not shared by many people throughout much of the world. Rosemary Radford Ruether describes the problem well.

> The argument that feminism is an expression of Western cultural imperialism and is inappropriate for women of the non-Western world has emerged in recent years as a major rhetorical rebuttal to the globalization of the movement for women's rights. I first encountered this argument in 1990 when I was traveling and lecturing in South Africa. I was speaking to a group of African women church workers in the Bantu "homeland" of Transkei. One African man was present, an Anglican priest dressed in impeccably tailored black clericals and speaking in British-accented English, neither the dress, the religion, nor the language being, one would think, traditionally "African."
>
> When I finished my remarks about Christian feminism, its Biblical roots, and contemporary developments worldwide, this priest rose to his full height and said, "Such ideas may be fine in the West, but they are completely contrary to our African culture." Fortunately, I had been primed with a good response by a friend of mine, an African woman sociologist. "Well," I replied, "you might say that racism is a part of traditional white culture. Would you say that you can't challenge white racism because it is a part of white culture?" The African women tittered, and the priest sat down, glaring.[19]

Although Ruether is wary of postmodern skepticism, her strategic response to the cross-cultural conflicts in values is one that I share: "Perhaps it is time for Western feminists to spend less time attacking concepts of human rights grounded in human nature and more time making them more credible across cultures."[20] What leads us to see that women have equal rights? Rather than simply proclaiming this as a universal good to those who do not agree that it is a universal truth, what are more effective arguments and political strategies?

My approach to multicultural education is decidedly postmodern. Although I do focus on the need for human rights, I do so not because these rights are either mandates from a source outside history or the natural concomitants of human nature. Social structures that acknowledge the rights of diverse groups of people are not the natural expressions of human essence, but a construct. Vibrant, pluralistic, self-critical, open-ended communities and relationships do exist. Although there are people who seek security in enclaves of like-minded people, others are energized by the play of like-mindedness and differences, energized by the play of similarity and nonhomogeneity, and find that life is richer because of the shock of the new, the charge of having basic assumptions questioned, the jolt of seeing the world in new ways. To some of us, having our pretensions punctured and errors exposed is more stimulating of laughter and creative thought, than merely seeing the gaps, inconsistencies, and errors in other's beliefs, analyses, and strategies.

I turn to multicultural education because I think democracy is a wager, an experiment, an effort to see if it is possible on a large scale for people to define themselves without demonizing and self-righteousness. Democracy, then, is not a given aspect of human nature but a structure that has to be created anew in each generation. Multicultural education is the practice of creating democracy, a practice of creating the type of intersubjectivity, of accountability that can enable people to learn from each others' differences, that can enable people to see oppression and do something to end it.

To say that our identities as individuals, cultures, communities, are multiple and changing, is not to say that there is no self or that there is no national or cultural identity. I see multicultural education as the process of understanding and participating deliberately in the process of individual, cultural, and national identity formations. Multicultural education is, thus, a self-critical "technology of the self." It challenges other technologies of the self, those based on exclusion of others, on demonizing and scapegoating. My project has been informed by Foucault's analyses of the processes by which the self is socially created, by his analyses of technologies of the self: "[By] studying madness and psychiatry, crime and punishment, I have tried to show how we have indirectly constituted ourselves through the exclusion of some others: criminals, mad people, and so on. And now my present work deals with the questions: How did we directly constitute our identity through some ethical techniques of the self which developed through antiquity down to now?"[21] Foucault saw the alternative as another technology of the self and not the discovery of human essence. He was wary, as I am, of any system of ethics or education that proposes to found itself on a supposedly universally true understanding of human nature, of the interactions of individuality and community. "What I am afraid of about humanism is that it presents a certain form of our ethics as a universal model for any kind of freedom. I think that there are more secrets, more possible freedoms, and more inventions in our future than we can imagine in humanism as it is dogmatically represented on every side of the political rainbow: the Left, the Center, the Right."[22]

What happens if we take this critique of humanism into our work in multicultural education? Multicultural education becomes not the pedagogy of a universally valid way of being human, but the opening of spaces for interaction, for accountability, invention, and critique. Our goal as educators is not to inculcate the right way of being human; our goal is to foster politically accountable and engaged, creative, and open-ended communities. Our analyses of the ways that gender, race, and class identities have been constructed opens the space for action and creativity. As Foucault states, "All my analyses are against the idea of universal necessities in human existence. They show the arbitrariness of institutions and which space of freedom we can still enjoy and how many changes can still be made."[23] The result, then, is not giving people a specific program for the future, but opening the space in which specific programs can be created, implemented, evaluated, rejected, and or worked with as the foundation of other programs.

For a rather long period, people have asked me to tell them what will happen and to give them a program for the future. We know very well that, even with the best intentions, those programs become a tool, an instrument of oppression. Rousseau, lover of freedom, was used in the French Revolution to build up a model of social oppression. Marx would be horrified by Stalinism and Leninism. My role—and that is too emphatic a word—is to show people that they are much freer than they feel, that people accept as truth, as evidence, some themes which have been built up at a certain moment during history, and that this so-called evidence can be critiqued and destroyed. To change something in the minds of people—that's the role of an intellectual.[24]

Behind this reading of the self is feminist and postmodern theory.[25] The application of postmodern theory to education emerges from concerns with liberation. Beginning with the work of Paulo Freire, many educators have explored the role of schooling in fostering critical political analysis and individual and group empowerment. Peter McLaren, for example, points to the resistance and creativity implicit in what appears to be the recalcitrance and self-defeating rebellion of working-class students. McLaren and Henry Giroux both extend the concern of Freire for liberation by examining the multiplicity of forms of oppression and the dangers and ambiguities of resistance.[26]

I see multicultural education as a practice of deconstruction, from which we can see both the value and limits of the work of deconstruction. The value of this approach lies in learning to see multiplicity and to see the ways in which identity is shaped by constitutive contradictions rather than by simple unequivocal characteristics.

The practice of multicultural education has something to add to deconstruction as well. What do we do after seeing multiplicity and contradictions? Merely pointing them out, denouncing them, is relatively meaningless. It may give the one denouncing a feeling of superiority, but it does nothing to change the practices so criticized. Multicultural education takes critique and moves from it to action, to the creation of different identities and different possibilities of response.

Let me develop these points in more detail. Many critics argue that deconstructionist philosophers deny the existence of the self. They point to Lyotard's claim that the self "does not amount to much" and Foucault's announcement of the "disappearance of man." Dickens states, "These researchers and others do not so much deny the existence of the self as they seek to re-situate it in light of the destabilizing tendencies they detect in contemporary mass-mediated societies."[27] Multicultural education is the practice of resituating the self without grounding the self in a universally true essence, or an absolute foundation.

Multicultural education does not "make sense" of the fragmentary and contradictory narratives that constitute individual, national, and group identities. The challenge of multicultural education, why it requires work on so many registers (conceptual, emotional, political, and physical), is that we must act, we must decide, we must evaluate, in a world that does not make sense. Multicultural education helps us act within this nondualistic world view, this recognition that, while we can use reason, our reason itself is fragmentary and the consequences of the use of that reason exceed our imaginative and speculative grasp. Multicultural education provides the tools to play the contradictions of individual and group identities without succumbing to either the illusion of certainty and control or the self-indulgent exercise of unaccountable and uncritical self-affirmation.

From the perspective of multicultural education, the current "identity crisis in family, economy, polity, race and gender relations" offers immense possibilities for creativity and well-being.[28] Identities are being challenged because of the ways in which they have justified various forms of oppressions—gender relations that defined men as leaders and foundational and women as merely supporters, our value dependent on our usefulness to men. White has meant superior to people of color. There are other components of white identity, to be sure, but it is the challenge to this component of white identity that leads to both crisis and opportunity.[29]

Emilie Townes provides a succinct account of both the promise of postmodernism and its danger at this time of political and cultural conflict. How do we address the search for security and control within resurgent fundamentalism? How do we challenge globalizing cultural identities that mask significant power differences between political and cultural groups? Townes argues that the concern of postmodern theorists for "plurality, particularity, locality, context, the social location of thought, and serious questioning of universal knowledge" can "provide a way for many to think their way into concrete knowledge of and contact with African American realities."[30] She claims that there is a convergence between postmodern concerns and the work of African American theorists.

> Black writers have provided a way into the bounty of Black life in the United States. Their work has fed (and has been nourished by) African American intellectuals as well as folks like Miss Nora and Brother Hemphill. The growing body of Black voices in our sociocultural matrix makes it difficult to maintain modernist protestations toward universality. More than ever before, we are challenged to consider the radical nature of particularity as foundational for ethical reflection.[31]

While valuing postmodern thought as an attempt to encounter 'Otherness,' Townes points to the dangers of solipsism, romanticization, and trivialization when our analysis stops too soon.

> Postmodern discourse and analysis that obscures the true diversity of life in the United States for Black Americans collapses African Americans into one grand master narrative. This narrative makes no distinction between the legacy of lynching in the United States, issues and concerns of Blacks in the rual South, or the rise of the Black cultural elite. Black folk become one dark stroke across the landscape of hegemonic discourse. The promise of postmodernism fails its liberative agenda. The call by Baby Suggs to love our hearts is a pithy reminder that particularity is more than an abstract construct of philosophical colloquy. Particularity, historicity, locality, and context all represent human beings. Concrete material existence and abstraction can and should meet in postmodernism.[32]

As Emilie Townes reminds us, "wholeness demands the whole truth—our lives are complex and have layers of experience in each moment."[33] This "wholeness" can be lost in the abstractions of people who belong to culturally and politically dominant groups; it can also be lost by those who have been defined as "Other."

> We make ourselves the oppositional Other, we turn to forms of self-hatred and self-destruction. Instead of critiquing and then working to eradicate notions of individualism, we forget our African past and seek to establish our lives as separate from one another. To recognize the differences in the socioeconomic structure of Black life does not mean that African Americans are free to cut those who are not in our social class or gender adrift from our lives. To divorce civil rights from environmental concerns is to live in a deadly dualism in which there will be no air to breathe. To practice historicla amnesia about the legacy of lynching in the United States is to doom all of us to find new material to construct postmodern nooses.[34]

What does it take to avoid historical amnesia? What does it take to see the "whole truth," these "truths" that are the effects of lies: lynching, rape, subjugation, and exploitation, all justified by the lies of white supremacy, male superiority, and the impossibility of re-ordering the world? In her poetry as well as her analytical work, Townes calls us from abstraction and grounds us in the pain and longing that lead us to seek new forms of connection, more responsible and creative ways of acting economically and politically.

> memories so old
>   time has forgot them
> memories so old
>   they sear my soul
> memories so old
>   the world has gone after
> memories so old
>   they wrest my heart from tomorrows
> such memories cut deep
> such memories die hard

such memories maim
such memories are lies
...
such memories need a God
   of breath by breath love[35]

Where Townes turns to "a God of breath," I turn to human connections of accountability and creativity, and see multicultural education as one means of fostering resilient, honest, self-critical, vital, and creative forms of community. Within multicultural education, we examine how people are constituted socially and how people act in response to the many forces that shape our identities. How do we respond to our cultures' definitions of individual and group identity? How do we interpret and respond to depictions of our identities in literature, television, movies, advertising, religious texts, and public policy? We examine how cultural texts are created and how they are "read," how they influence people's lives. Stuart Hall delineates three forms of response to such texts: the dominant, the negotiated, and the oppositional. Dickens provides a concise summary of these three responses:

> While the dominant code in a cultural text reflects relatively straight-forwardly the dominant cultural ideology, the negotiated code reflects the dominant ideology only in a more situationally restricted fashion. In the oppositional code, messages are reinterpreted in terms of an alternative normative framework, opening the door for a more critical political interpretation of a film, or book, or scientific treatise. In so doing, oppositional readings aim to "expose the ideological or political meanings that circulate within the text, particularly those which hide or displace racial, class, ethnic and gender biases."[36]

I see multicultural education as taking these codes to another level of action and reflection. Let's begin with the third; what do we do *after* we see the political meanings and biases within culture? What do we put in place of those definitions? How do we check for unforeseen biases and limits in new definitions? How do we learn to respect that which is outside our control—either conceptually or politically? What intellectual and emotional skills, even what physical resources, are required for such respect?

The condition of work for justice, what enables challenging unjust social structures is not guilt, is not duty, is not sacrifice for some higher ideal. The foundation of self-critical, open-ended, life-sustaining work for justice is beauty. In her description of what non–Native Americans can learn from Native American traditions, Carol Lee Sanchez writes of the daily meditation on the beauty of the natural world—choosing a tree or plant and being attentive to it. What happens as we immerse ourselves in the play of light and shadow, the shades of green, the texture of leaf and bark, the feel of breezes, the shifting conditions of humidity and temperature, the change of seasons? Sanchez claims that "focusing on destructive forces all the time causes feelings of despair and, too often, a sense of powerlessness to do anything to change these dreadful circumstances."[37] What does she offer instead? A way of life found in all North American tribes, and called the Beauty Way by the Navaho: "When we seek the beauty and wonder of creation, creation responds by bringing more beauty and wonder for us to be glad about and thankful for."[38] It is beauty and wonder that inspires our work for justice:

> Center yourself in the region where you make your home and introduce yourself to the spirits of your place. Greet the plant, creature, mineral, wind, water, earth, and sky spirits. Make a song to them. Do this in a sacred manner.... If ... you will attune yourself to your homeplace, and if you make it a point to acknowledge your nonhuman surroundings on a daily basis (several times a day, preferably), your environment will begin to respond to you according to your thoughts. Welcome all your relatives into your immediate family. Approach each day in a sacred manner and with a healthy sense of humor. Our relatives will help us if we ask them to help. Our relatives will forgive us if we ask for their forgiveness and make a serious commitment not to repeat our previous mistakes.... If we all open our hearts and minds to this rich legacy, we may discover many creative solutions to our ecological dilemmas.[39]

The source of work for justice is beauty; being grateful for the gift of life, honoring it, celebrating it, playing our part in this chaotic, glorious adventure.

III. ACCOUNTABILITY, NOT GUILT

Multicultural education moves beyond the dualistic game, the easy satisfactions so characteristic of much leftist literature. Rather than merely denouncing oppressive structures and oppressors, the people who implement those structures and benefit from them, we look at what enables people to even see oppression as oppression, and then, at what enables us to change oppressive structures.[40]

One approach often taken with groups and people seen as oppressive seems to me counterproductive. Leftists often call on people in power to give up their power, to renounce privilege, and to give power to those who have been marginalized. The focus of education, of diversity training, is on guilt: making the oppressors realize their behaviors, feel guilty because of it, and then stop doing it. Typical activities include ones in which people are tricked into exposing their complicity in oppression—e.g. whites being asked to identify things they like about being white, and then being told that what they have identified is white privilege—resulting in them feeling ashamed, exposed as oppressors who enjoy the benefits of racial oppression.[41]

I think another approach is more conducive to social change. Rather than being asked to feel guilty and then to give up power, privileged people, "oppressors," are challenged to use their privilege, and thereby put it at risk, in the interest of justice. This brings about a threefold evolution: (1) those in power identify factors within their culture that lead to justice; (2) they are connected with people hurt by injustice, see their dignity and strength, and come to respect and learn from them; and (3) they learn of people who were "oppressors" but who came to use their power as allies for social justice.

How do we forthrightly acknowledge and then work creatively with the strengths and weakness of our racial identities? Take, for example, the following description of white culture developed by Judith Katz.

THE COMPONENTS OF WHITE CULTURE: VALUES AND BELIEFS[42]

Rugged Individualism:
Individual is primary unit
Individual has primary responsibility
Independence and autonomy highly
     valued and rewarded
Individual can control environment

Competition:
Winning is everything
Win/lose dichotomy

Action Orientation:
Must master and control nature
Must always do something about
     a situation
Pragmatic/utilitarian view of life

Decision Making:
Majority rule when Whites have
     power
Hierarchical
Pyramid structure

Communication:
Standard English
Written tradition
Direct eye contact
Limited physical contact
Controlled emotions

Time:
Adherence to a rigid time schedule
Time is viewed as a commodity

Holidays:
Based on Christian religion
Based on White history and male
     leaders

History:
Based on European immigrants'
     experience in United States
Romanticize war

Protestant Work Ethic:
Working hard brings success

Progress and Future Orientation:
Plan for future
Delayed gratification
Value continual improvement and
     progress

Emphasis on Scientific Method:
Objective, rational, linear thinking
Cause and effect relationships
Quantitative emphasis
Dualistic thinking

Status and Power:
Measured by economic possessions
Credentials, titles, and positions
Believe "own" system
Believe better than other systems
Owning goods, space, property

Family Structure:
Nuclear family is the ideal social unit
Man is breadwinner and the head of
     the household
Woman is homemaker and subordi-
     nate to the husband
Patriarchal structure

Aesthetics:
Music and art based on European
     cultures
Women's beauty based on blonde,
     blue-eyed, thin, young
Men's attractiveness based on athletic
     ability, power, economic status

Religion:
Belief in Christianity
No tolerance for deviation from single
     god concept

The problem with this list is its lack of nuance. There is no differentiation of aspects of white culture that are cause for pride, aspects that can be utilized in the service of racial justice, and those that are destructive and worthy of critique. Katz does not include, for example, the ambiguities of the American culture of voluntary associations, our tendencies to come together to resolve common problems.[43] How do we acknowledge the limits of volunteerism, yet at the same time value and expand the power of this commitment to working for the good of one's community?

It is as important that we value the culture of white students as we value the culture of students of color. We begin our workshop on racial diversity, for example, by helping whites identify the elements in our culture that provide the resources for both seeing injustice and using our power to implement racial equality.[44] Just as the oppressed or marginalized are more than victimization, the dominant are more than the structures of domination and conscious or unwitting privilege and exclusion. Our ground for hope is not merely the cries of the oppressed, but also the ability of the dominant to see injustice and work with the oppressed to create alternatives to unjust social structures.

The goal for all people within multicultural education, for "oppressor" and "oppressed," is empowerment and accountability. Just as the oppressed are empowered to resist injustice and create just structures, so oppressors are challenged to use their power for justice. There is more to be gained through acting for justice than in maintaining individual or group dominance: there is a richer self, a more rewarding group identity to be gained through open-ended pluralism than through tightly defined exclusivity. The challenge is not one of sacrifice—sacrificing power, access, and group identity—but rather of constituting another form of group and self-identity, using power to facilitate diversity and ongoing self-critique rather than to maintain control.

If we focus on accountability and not guilt, what follows? First, a crucial component of accountability is simply seeing difference as difference, acknowledging that there are people whose experiences and insights differ from one's own. Second, difference can be perceived as intriguing, as a challenge and a resource, and not as a threat. Third, the use of one's power for justice, even in the face of repeated defeats, can be deeply satisfying. Molly Ivins describes such a sensibility in her account of members of the Texas state legislature, who, against all odds, persist in work for human rights.

> For the past twenty years, the House has harbored a liberal opposition numbering somewhere between twenty and forty. They boast the longest unbroken string of defeats this side of the Philadelphia Phillies, but are *toujours gai*.[45]

A key assumption in multicultural education is that oppression, bias, exclusion, exploitation, and discrimination hurt all—both those victimized or targeted for such actions and those who supposedly benefit from them. My wager is that this whiteness, constituted by imputed superiority to people of color, this masculinity, founded on control of women, is less rich, less joyous, less rewarding than a whiteness and a maleness constituted by respect for self and others.[46] It is easy to make the case that the world is better for the oppressed when injustice is ended, but I wager that life is better for those privileged as well.

Why do I say this? Because the self is intrinsically unstable. Self-identity, group identity are continuously in formation, having to be re-enacted, reframed. The self- and group identities constituted by domination and control are not only unstable, but also marked by insecurity and fear, by the malaise that comes from knowing that one's identity is constituted through coercion and violence, that it is contested by those who rebel against its privileges and constraints.

Starhawk, in a critique of the men's movement, makes a helpful distinction between spiritual malaise and oppression:

> Oppression is what the slaves suffer; malaise is what happens to the slaveowners whose personalities are warped and whose essential humanity is necessarily undermined by their position. Malaise and oppression are both painful but they are not comparable. The necessary first step in the cure for what ails the slaveowner is to free the slaves.[47]

The transformation, and thus healing of such a self and such selves, requires seeing that the domination through which it actualizes itself is ridden with the assumptions of class, race, and gender privileges. The transformation of such selves requires alternate technologies of the self, technologies predicated upon interdependence, accountability, and open and acknowledged conflict, rather than upon hidden, denied, and naturalized conflict.

How do we hold each other accountable? How do we criticize each other? Many groups acknowledge the destructive effects of some forms of criticism. Leaders of any group, for example, often become the target of intense, misplaced critique. If a group expects their leaders, because they are from marginalized groups, to escape hierarchical behavior, they may feel betrayed and outraged by mistakes and abuses of power on the part of leaders. Groups often move from idolizing leaders to seeing them as incompetent, attacking them and trying to remove them from office. How do we escape this cycle? Some groups do not allow attacks on leaders. I think a better approach, however, given that leaders, like all of us, do make mistakes and do abuse power, is to lower the threshold of critique. Rather than seeing mistakes and abuses of power as a sign of the fundamental unworthiness of a leader, see it as being human, and the reason we need regular mechanisms for critique and response to that critique. Critique then becomes a means of group cohesion, a way of telling stories and solving problems together. Multicultural education, then, enables civility by normalizing criticism. Not only is the amount of criticism increased, but also the energy and the impact of criticism is shifted. Rather than criticism destroying a community or a relationship, it can be an invitation to a deeper relationship, part of the process of creating a stronger community.

Vivian Paley describes the process of creating a larger community, a self constituted by respectful interaction with diverse groups, in *Kwanzaa and Me*. In this book she wrestles with the challenge of creating a racially inclusive community. She sets forward an African American critique of white attempts at integration, and the desire of many African American parents to educate their children in all-black schools to give them a foundation of self-respect so they can then be a confident and secure member of a multiracial society, drawing on community support to challenge continued racism.[48]

Paley takes these critiques seriously, and uses them as an opening to a deeper relationship, trying to discern the ways that the classroom continues to devalue the experience and culture of children of color. She makes the exploration of difference a central and ongoing dimension of her teaching. She tells the children a series of stories, using characters of different races in nonstereotypical roles. She invites the parents of students to visit the classroom and tell stories about their lives, making sure that the children from nondominant cultures are fully included. Just as the parents tell stories, the children tell theirs. What, then, according to Paley, creates community? Not uniformity, but "The telling of our stories and the solving of our social problems."[49]

The wager that informs multicultural education, is that ending oppression benefits the oppressor as well as the oppressed. Our task then, is to appeal to oppressors to change, not out of guilt, but out of vitality, pride, and joy—wholeheartedly embracing a way of life that builds on what is best in being human, even what we value about being white, or what men value about masculinity. In living this way, there are costs, but the costs are not adequately described as sacrifice. What is given up—racial privilege or male domination—is of less value than what is gained—being enriched by working with and learning from women and from people of color.

IV. CELEBRATING OUR POWER TO BE AGENTS OF SOCIAL JUSTICE: A POSTMODERN MODEL OF DIVERSITY TRAINING

One of our major challenges as a nation is to learn to be accountable for our multiple identities: to recognize the ways in which we have power and then use it well, to recognize the ways in which we and other groups are denied equity, opportunity, and access.

I describe now a model of diversity training that has four goals: recognizing systemic power imbalances, acknowledging the power held by one's own group, gaining the courage to use that power for justice, and discovering how to learn from conflict. This process can be used in a wide range of settings, from a single workshop to a semester-long class. I go into it in some detail, focusing on the issue of racism, although the process can be readily used with other forms of oppression and exclusion.

The first stage of the workshop is a modification of the guidelines taught by the Equity Institute. We begin by acknowledging our purpose—to become more effective in our work for racial justice. In order to do this work, we need to keep in mind a set of assumptions and guidelines. I present the previously described assumptions about democracy, accountability, and change, and then move on to a consideration of guidelines for our work together in this workshop.

First, it is crucial to know that this workshop, or this class, is not a safe space. We are discussing volatile issues and there will be areas of profound disagreement. We enter this discussion as individuals and as groups with radically different histories and experiences. There are power differentials between us as individuals and between the groups we represent. In trying to learn from each other, in learning how to work together, it is essential that we acknowledge that this is painful, difficult, and possibly exhilarating work. We do not know if we can trust each other. We are afraid of offending each other and we are afraid of being offended. In this workshop we *are* likely to offend, disappoint, and surprise each other, and we will probably be hurt and challenged. We are not, therefore, in a safe space. However, we are in a space for learning, a space in which we may learn how to work with conflict and how to learn from each other. This workshop is not a haven from the external world of injustice and mistrust but rather a place of learning how to work within that world for more justice, for more cooperation and respect.

Given the importance and volatility of our task, I offer the following guidelines and then ask the group to add others. These guidelines help us as we work at the edge of our comprehension of self and group identity:

• freedom to leave

• respect

- risk-taking

- confidentiality

- ouch, no zaps

The first guideline: anyone may leave at any time. This is difficult and often painful work. If it becomes too intense, feel free to leave for a few moments or to leave the workshop entirely. The second guideline: respect. By respect we do not mean agreement, but taking someone so seriously that you ask why they think as they do. Respect means recognizing that people have reasons for their behaviors and beliefs and that we need to engage those reasons in order to work together effectively, or in order to change behaviors we see as harmful or ideas we see as wrong. Even if the reasons seem wrong, we need to understand and gauge their power and hold. Are these lightly held ideas, easily changed with different information? Are they lightly held ideas, and ones we see as right, but in need of being deepened in order to withstand the challenges of implementing them? Or are these deeply held convictions, part of how an individual or a group defines itself?

The third guideline: take risks. We are taking risks in this environment, trying out ideas, analyses, and strategies. What we say now we may not believe in ten minutes, much less in ten years. The fourth guideline is confidentiality. While reflection on personal experiences is an intrinsic part of the alchemical process, part of conjuring alternative forms of individual and group identity, such reflection is often best done privately. In all classes and workshops, self-reflection is elicited: self-disclosure, however, is never mandatory and always optional.

There are often good reasons for maintaining privacy. Within the classroom, and especially within diversity workshops in a business setting, there are degrees of intimacy and differences in power. These are not safe spaces and we do our students and colleagues a disservice if we pretend that they are. Personal disclosure may be risky or inappropriate. In my workshops, therefore, I combine the need for privacy and self-reflection. I ask people to reflect on their own experiences, but when it comes to discussion, I offer the option of speaking from a more generalized point of view. For example, in workshops on racial diversity with teachers, I ask them to reflect on two sorts of experiences: first, their own early memories of experiencing race as a way of characterizing people; and, after reflecting on that memory, the aspects of racial stereotyping, prejudice, and bigotry that they see in their classrooms.[50] When it is time for discussion, they may talk about their own experiences, or they may focus on what is happening in their classroom. If they do decide to talk about their lives, confidentiality is crucial. In the class, people may very well tell stories about themselves that they would not feel free to tell anywhere else. Any personal stories, then, should not be repeated outside the class. This applies to work in dyads or small groups as well: If someone recounts an incident in a small group, it is up to them, not another, to tell the story to the whole group.

There is one exception to the guideline: participants are free to repeat anything I, or any other facilitator, say outside of class. Why the difference in confidentiality? I want the students to feel confident in sharing personal information and trying to make sense of it, but the facilitator's power as leader needs to be checked. Participants deserve explicit permission to critically evaluate what we are doing and saying in our workshops.

The fifth guideline is "ouch, no zaps." Since we are dealing with complex issues, ones that are new to many of us, I tell people to expect that we will say something offensive and that others will as well. As soon as that happens, say "ouch." Do not wait until you are so angry that you have to explode. By "no zaps" I mean no name calling or denunciations, so rather than denouncing someone as a racist, simply say "ouch." Also, express your discontent even if you do not have it formulated in clear theoretical terms. If we understand why what we said was offensive, we can simply apologize and move on. If we do not understand, we ask for more information.

How else are we going to learn? As long as all of my friends and colleagues were white, I thought only other white people were racist. Not until I worked closely with people of color did I have people point out how my behavior and attitudes were prejudiced and racist.

After the discussion of the assumptions and guidelines, we go on to an exercise that helps people see the reality of oppression: the relationships between oppression by race, class, gender, and sexual orientation; and the possibilities for social transformation. This exercise works as well with groups who do not believe there is any oppression as with groups who are already well aware of its depth and complexity. I learned the exercise from Dr. William Jones, director of black studies at Florida State University.[51] He has used it to work for racial inclusion in both the United States and South Africa. I have modified the exercise, correlating it with Kanter's theory of proportions and the Equity Institute's analysis of allies and empowered groups.

Exercise:

Divide into groups of five. Ask each person to identify one institution in their hometown that is powerful. This must be an institution that they know about personally—they know who is involved in it; they know about its impact. I give an example: I grew up in a farming community and the bank was definitely a powerful institution. People usually mention institutions like developers and realtors, specific large businesses, city government, police force, school board, churches, and the military.

I list the institutions on the board. I then ask people to name who has the most power in that institution—i.e., bank president and shareholders rather than tellers. Next, I ask people to identify that powerful person by race, gender, class, and presumed sexual orientation.

The answers are, not surprisingly, usually primarily white, upper or middle class, presumably heterosexual males. Quite often there are a few women or people of color. This is systemic power. We discuss then the shifts in the last thirty years in access to decision-making and institutional power.

In order to demonstrate that these results are not a fluke, I ask the group to name any institutions that they know of, either locally or nationally, controlled by African Americans. This leads to a discussion of the degree of power held by African Americans in sports, television, movies, and music, and to a discussion of the degree of power held by African American mayors, representatives, university administrators, etc. Other institutions named are black churches and colleges. We quickly see that even where there are larger numbers of African

Americans, e.g., sports and music, the ownership of professional teams and of record companies is predominantly white.

Then I ask, "Are there any institutions controlled by African Americans under which whites have to live?"

The answer here, again, is stark. Aside from a few mayors and police chiefs, there are none.

Given the analysis of their own experience, the group is now ready to examine statistical information on race and gender disparity in income and leadership in business and politics.[52] After examining current statistics, we look at definitions of power and of racism. I point out that those who have easy access to decision-making positions can be either agents or allies: either agents of maintaining exclusivity and control (most often unwittingly, but sometimes consciously and deliberately) or allies, actively using their (our) power to make decision making accessible to all people. Those who are under-represented in decision making can be either targeted or empowered. Certain groups are targeted for bias, discrimination, and oppression, and those same groups (African Americans, women, other people of color) are far more than victims, our history more than the history of oppression, our culture more than a culture of self-doubt or even resistance. Oppressed groups do have a measure of cultural and political power that needs to be recognized, understood and celebrated.[53]

What this part of the exercise illustrates is the nature of institutional power. The next step is focusing on how institutions become racist. We distinguish between three forms of racism: personal, cultural, and institutional. Personal racism is either prejudice (stereotypes based on ignorance and amenable to correction through education) or bigotry (an emotional commitment to ignorance). Prejudice or bigotry plus institutional power equals institutional racism. Cultural racism is the assumption that white or European culture is the norm (e.g., flesh-colored Band-aids that are only peach or beige, focus on European art and classical music, ignoring other classical forms of music, like jazz). This segment helps people move from thinking of racism as some sort of vague "bad thing" to seeing it as a phenomenon that takes different forms and can be responded to concretely and directly.

Having demonstrated, through a comparative analysis of the student's own awareness of differential access and statistical data on income levels and representation in government, the disparities in power in our society, we continue with an examination of how to play those disparities. Given their concentration in positions of institutional and cultural power, do white, upper-middle-class, heterosexual men feel powerful? Why or why not? As the statistics demonstrate, as the students know from their own lives, there has been change. Although women and people of color are still not included in proportion to our numbers, there have been shifts. How do we work with those shifts; what are effective ways of increasing access and reallocating power?

The barriers to sustained work for social change vary depending on the level of social change achieved. Rosabeth Moss Kanter has described what happens to women when we first enter a predominantly male workplace as managers, leaders, and decision-makers. She speaks of two types of organizations, "skewed" and "tilted." In a skewed workplace, women constitute less than 15 percent of the decision makers. In a tilted workplace, women comprise up to 35 percent of those who are managers. Kanter found that in the skewed environment, women were perceived by themselves and others stereotypically, and they tended to either overachieve or underachieve. In a tilted environment, women began to exercise the power of self-definition. Women viewed themselves and were viewed by others less stereotypically. Also, the achievement of women was more balanced, reflecting range and proportions more like that of men in the organization. Leola Johnson used Kanter's model to examine the power dynamics that accompany the formation of coalitions between black caucuses and women's caucuses in the newsroom.[54]

As formerly excluded groups gain influence and power, the dynamics of support and resistance shift. Within a skewed organization, some members of the dominant group are likely to be strong and effective allies, working with women or racial minorities to break barriers and bring the first people from different groups into the organization. When power shifts and there are more than token representatives of different groups, new forms of resistance emerge within the power elite. Those who were allies may find themselves defensive and resistant to further inclusion and to the impact of the inclusion achieved thus far. For, as the numbers increase, the power of naming shifts: the new groups not only begin to change how they name themselves and are defined by others but also challenge the normal codes of operation—what counts as business as usual, what the mission and focus of the organization should be. At this point, former allies may backtrack, feeling a loss of power, feeling a challenge to their power of naming.[55]

The dynamics of social change at each level vary and require differential work on psychological and sociological factors. Let's begin by thinking through the dynamics at work in a skewed organization. What is going on in regard to collective power relations—for those being included and for those doing the inclusion? In a skewed organization, the power balance between dominant and marginalized groups remains largely intact. The dominant group still sets the standards for admission, hiring, and promotion.

There is the danger that those who are allies will congratulate themselves on their positive relationships with a few minorities and not see the systemic power relations at play. They, we, are still setting the rules for who gets in and who advances once they are in, still setting the agenda of the organization. To help a few women or people of color fit into a skewed organization is an important task. It is good in itself—and it is also not enough. Those who are dominant may be choosing to admit and mentor only those people who are able to assimilate, thereby not gaining diversity that could lead to foundational critique and revisioning. The pattern is repeated in universities, in businesses, in political organizations: a few women or minorities— those most like the dominant group—are admitted, mentored, honored, given highly visible positions, often asked to serve on numerous committees, and consulted often; yet structural barriers remain.[56]

Within a skewed organization, the psychological pressure on token minorities, pressures stemming from sociological factors due to an imbalance of power, are immense. There is the conflicting pressure on the individual to maintain one's position within the organization and yet use that position to challenge stereotypes and oppressive structures. The problem is that, without collective support, without there being more minorities in the organization, such change is highly unlikely. Kanter recounts the patterns of people who are tokens either underachieving or overachieving—thriving because of the pressure or breaking.[57]

Now, what is the import of this? What difference can knowing these interrelated psychological and sociological factors make in our political work? For those of us who find ourselves to be tokens, the psychological task becomes one of finding group support outside the organization—realizing that our identity will be pulled in contradictory directions, and that we need regular and sustained grounding in, and support from, our own culture. We need spiritual and physical disciplines that enable endurance and patience, and the honesty of seeing the limits of what we can do. On the sociological side, we can realize that our primary effort is to put in place the conditions for structural change. Rather than thinking that individuals or a small group can change sexist advertising or the racist and sexist biases of a college curriculum, we should realize that systemic change requires numbers and work on increasing the number of women and people of color in decision-making positions.

What happens, then, when critical mass is reached? What happens when an organization is tilted toward equality? At this point, the balance of power is shifting, and further systemic change is possible, change in standards for admission, for promotion, changes in the mission of the organization, changes in how the organization sees itself as being accountable. Once again, there is a play of psychological and sociological factors. Those who are members of the dominant group, even staunch allies and mentors of people of color, must remain aware of the likely psychological impact of sociological change, of feeling threatened when they lose their power of naming. Rather than merely blaming those who resist further change, we must acknowledge that resistance. We can point out its grounding in unjust power relationships and provide the resources for individuals to make the shift. People need help in learning, practicing, and seeing nondominant ways of exercising power.

This analysis is sharply divergent from the typical leftist analysis of oppressors and oppression: people in power will never give up their power willingly; therefore, power must be taken from them. The issue is not giving up power but using it for different purposes (ending sexism and racism rather than maintaining individual and group wealth and influence) and being accountable to a larger group for the use of that power. How do our actions help or hinder the well-being of diverse groups of people? The key here is using power within a different frame of reference. Whites who are aware of the cost of racism can use our privilege to challenge other whites as individuals, and we can use our privilege to change structures, to put in place power relations that are more equitable.

There are psychological rewards and costs to participating in structural change. The costs are clear and often seem overwhelming. It is difficult for many whites (similarly many men) to admit that even in our work for justice we carry the conditioning of our group, and are, therefore, likely to replicate the very structures we are trying to replace.[58] This is not, however, cause for guilt or despair, but for accountability and openness to critique.

Being resilient, willing to take risks, to make mistakes and learn from them, comes from a combination of psychological and sociological factors. On the individual level, resources of spirituality, physical discipline (exercise of some sort), and music are essential. On the sociological side, belonging to a larger, more inclusive community is essential to sustain a differential use of privilege and access. Virginia Durr, longtime white civil rights activist, wrote of the costs of that work, naming her book *Outside the Magic Circle*. For a white woman to challenge racism was to step outside the bounds—and bonds and support—of the white community of friends, colleagues, and family.

> There were three ways for a well-brought-up Southern white woman to go. She could be the actress, playing out the stereotype of the Southern belle. Gracious to the "colored help," flirtatious to her powerful father-in-law, and offering a sweet, winning smile to the world. In short, going with the flow. If she had a spark of independence, or worse, creativity, she would go crazy.

> Or she could be the rebel. She could step outside the magic cir-
> cle, abandon privilege, and challenge this way of life. Ostracism,
> bruises of all sorts, and defamation would be her lot. Her reward
> would be a truly examined life and a world she would otherwise
> never have known.[59]

For those of us who are "oppressors," challenging those we love, challenging the group to which we belong, is a difficult task, requiring psychological strength and a change in collective support and in group membership. Rather than stepping "outside the magic circle," we can step inside another magic circle, one enriched by more people, more insights, and more perspectives. Thus we seek inclusion and diversity not out of guilt or to appease a strident constituency, but because we genuinely want to learn from other people and other groups.

For the oppressed or marginalized side of the equation, what are our psychological and sociological tasks as we move into a tilted organization and into positions of power? When we are aware of the sociological dynamics at work, the psychological impact of these challenges is not as devastating, For example, knowing Kanter's theory, it is not surprising that there will be greater levels of resistance, even from former allies, once we reach the tilting point. When we know this is likely to be the case, it is easier to accept it, to mobilize energy to work with it, and not waste time bemoaning the fact that another level and type of organization is required. It is easier to work with the resistance of former allies when we see it as part of a pattern, part of the challenge of gaining access to decision making, and not as a sign of ultimate defeat or their intractable resistance to change. If we are aware of the sociological factors that lead allies to become resistant, we can avoid demonizing them, writing them off as implacable enemies. We can construe their opposition as temporary, amenable therefore to intervention and change.

As we gain political power, we must be aware of the psychological dynamics by which those of us who have been marginalized defeat ourselves. Work for social justice is hampered if we fail to realize that the psychological skills/tasks of using power are quite different from the psychological/emotional habits that often accompany gaining power. In order to use power, not just get attention or get access, in order to build institutions and implement policies and not just criticize them, we have to break out of the dualistic oppressor/oppressed mindset and see the capacities for justice among "oppressors," the capacity for injustice among the "oppressed."

Multicultural education is deeply disturbing, as disturbing to the myths of a common culture as it is to the myths of a revolutionary vanguard. It is also profoundly rewarding and exhilarating, a rush of creative energy that takes us out of the paralyzing trap of endlessly denouncing and analyzing forms of injustice and oppression. We can do so much more. The first step is to recognize that social cohesion is created by contact, by working with other people, and does not require uniformity or total agreement. The second step is focusing on the power we have and using it to create relationships of mutuality and respect. Universal human solidarity is not our birthright, not a gift, not an essence, but a task.

5

Ethics Without Virtue

When I first heard that Derrida had said, in response to questions about apartheid, that the basis of an ethical and political critique of that system was aesthetics—I was appalled.[1] Reduce ethics to aesthetics? What an outrage! Could there be any more blatant manifestation of distancing, of privilege, of the inability of the elite to take seriously the suffering of others?

Now, after more years of work as an activist, after rereading Bonhoeffer, after learning more about Caribbean literature and Haitian Vodou, I am more sympathetic to Derrida's response. Aesthetics is a key component of ethics. At crucial junctures in shaping our responses to both the challenges of interpersonal decency and systemic injustice, it is as much a matter of style as it is courage to act well, to act honorably, to act with creativity and accountability. Let me give an example, a circuitous route into what I mean by style and by aesthetics.

As a gentile, raised in a Christian culture, the Holocaust has always been, for me, the test of Christianity's claims about being good for people. The Holocaust is also a test of socialism, of liberalism, of any form of secular progressive thought. The fundamental question for any gentile is, how did we do that? The systematic torture, brutalization, and murder of six million human beings? Why didn't we stop it? How did our reason, faith, and ethics fail to such a horrific, unfathomable extent?

In thinking about the Holocaust and moral accountability, I find it crucial to keep in mind Fackenheim's discussion of the ways in which people avoid the moral challenge of the Holocaust. The first way is to say that it was the fault of a few evil people; we then see the Nazis as somehow fundamentally different than us, as an evil force that has nothing to do with us and our systems of faith, reason, and morals.

> Two opposite forms of escapism must be avoided. We cannot make the Nazi murderers into a species separate from all humanity, with the results that their actions become a product of (historical, genetic, or medical) fate; that their post-war return to ordinary existence becomes a mystery; and that neither the first nor the second has any relation to ourselves. And we cannot, on the grounds that all men are sinners, dissolve or weaken the distinction between those who might have done it and those who did it. This latter is especially tempting to Christians. Thus, e.g., in William Styron's Holocaust novel Sophie's Choice, Josef Mengele, the notorious Auschwitz SS doctor ... becomes "Dr. Jemand von Niemand"—Dr. Anyone and No one.[2]

I have always thought of the Holocaust in quite different terms, as something we Christians did. As Gushee points out in *Righteous Gentiles,* less than 1 percent of the gentiles in Europe resisted the Holocaust; 99 percent included not just bystanders—paralyzed, enervated in the face of the death camps—but also those who participated directly in persecuting and killing Jews.[3]

But surely this participation was coerced: was it not a choice of survival? No, not always, not often. In *Ordinary Men,* Christopher Browning gives a chilling account of the decision to participate directly in murder. Ordinary men, not unusually anti-Semitic, were enlisted in a battalion to aid the Nazis in the murder of Jews. They were given the choice of participating or not. There were no "dire threats," no extreme pressures or sanctions, and yet most joined in the killing. Many were sickened, many were horrified, but they persisted in the murder.[4]

Of the 500 men in the battalion, about twelve took advantage of the battalion commander's explicit offer: "Any of the men who did not feel up to the task that lay before them could step out." By the end of the day, the offer having been made twice again, another twelve or so had quit participating in the killing; but then only because they had sickened of it, and not because of any ethical objections.[5] Many of those who murdered Jews were not demons; they were "ordinary men," people like us.[6]

Fackenheim claims that the ethical weight of the Holocaust can also be evaded through a quite different strategy. This time, instead of saying that "they" did it and separating ourselves from the "they," we say that "we" did it, which shows an inevitable weakness and cruelty that resides in all of us. Once again we have denial, but this time a denial that evades the possibility of choice, the possibility of being human in a way that fed resistance and not participation.[7] After all, many Jews and some gentiles—far too few to be sure, but some nonetheless—did resist.

What made the difference? What made resistance possible, and what can all of this have to do with something as ephemeral as style?

Dietrich Bonhoeffer gives us a good case study of resistance, ethics, courage and weakness. He was an upper-class German pastor who opposed Hitler and encouraged other Christians and gentiles to do the same. He was a leader in the formation of the Confessing Church and in international ecumenical circles. He helped Jews escape from Germany, and was part of a group of high-ranking military officers who tried to assassinate Hitler, stage a coup, and defeat and replace fascism. While in prison on charges of helping Jews escape, two of the planned assassination attempts failed, his role in the plot was discovered, and he was executed in April 1945.[8]

Bonhoeffer was an activist, a pastor, and a scholar. His letters from prison have been published, and he wrote on ethics and religion and society before his arrest. In his writings he tried to understand why so many good, decent, German Christians supported Hitler and/or refused to become involved in resistance. Christianity had a tradition that should have led to massive resistance—a tradition shaped by absolutes, by universal claims based not just on human reasoning, but also purportedly on divine revelation. In Christianity, the idea of divine authority should have led many Christians, and not just the few members of the Confessing Church, to affirm the Lordship of Christ over and against the authority of Hitler and the Third Reich.[9] Also central to Christian faith was a universal claim that all humans are in the image of God and a universally sanctioned ethic of self-sacrifice, as practiced by Jesus and advocated by him for all Christians: "No greater love hath this...." This ideal, that all people are made in the image of God, and the practice of sacrificial love should have led Christians to defend Jews. Against claims that to do so was to risk one's own life, what better challenge than the absolute injunction of self-sacrifice?

What vitiated these absolutes? One factor was the effectiveness of Nazi propaganda, exacerbating the demonizing of Jews that was already a part of Christian anti-Semitism. Jews were made the scapegoats for Germany's ills—depicted, quite successfully, as less than human, as outside the bonds of human obligation.[10] Bonhoeffer argued, however, that most Christians were not persuaded by Nazi propaganda. They knew what was happening to Jews and they knew it was wrong.[11] Given adequate knowledge and adequate moral evaluation of that knowledge, why did 99 percent either stand by or participate in dehumanization and murder? Bonhoeffer's answer: Folly, and a fear of moral ambiguity.[12]

Bonhoeffer defined folly as capitulation in the face of overweening power. Knowing the brutalization and murder of Jews was wrong, knowing that these horrors should be stopped, many were paralyzed by the power of Nazism, unable to imagine and carry out any forms of resistance. This paralysis was aggravated by what Bonhoeffer identified as an excessive sense of scruples—trying to remain morally pure while resisting evil.[13] Given the power of the Nazis, resistance was often covert and deception commonplace, an essential tool of resistance for those people who hid Jews and helped Jews escape. There were many layers of deception—lying to authorities, making false papers, lying to friends and neighbors.

Why, then, the failure to act? According to Bonhoeffer, the failure to act came from a fear of moral ambiguity. The moral ambiguity that characterized resistance was manifold. Any resistance was partial, its likely effects paltry, incommensurate with the outrages of genocide. Any attempt would save so few lives and there were so many lives being lost. There was also the ambiguity of not being able to predict the consequences of one's actions: would they be successful, would they bring harm to oneself and to one's family? Bonhoeffer highlighted a third aspect of the moral ambiguity of resistance: resisting fascism required acting in ways that were themselves immoral. To be moral, to save Jews, required lying and deception, it required breaking the law; it might even lead, as it did in the case of Bonhoeffer, to the plan to murder Hitler.[14]

Now, here is the key issue: what is the difference between accepting moral and political ambiguity in a way that is self-critical, and using ambiguity in a way that is self-justifying? Let's explore the alternatives. Imagine that we realize that moral choices are those in which one has to choose between principles. Furthermore, it is often impossible to predict if one's actions will do more harm than good or if the actions will be successful. Faced with these ambiguities, we might give up on moral reflection altogether: acting boldly, but without the pretense of being moral, without any attempt to think through actions and their impact on others. Action then becomes sheer impulse, whim, the arbitrary exercise of creativity and power.

Imagine another alternative. We can take ambiguity seriously, making a best choice, and then being willing to accept the consequences of that choice.[15] Basically, we become ready to clean up after ourselves, to reevaluate actions, all with the style of humor and openness to failure. The key here is not being paralyzed by either moral failure or by political actions that are ineffective. We can accept that we can only do our best, with a style of not expecting perfection or saintliness from ourselves and others. It is then easier to act in ambiguous situations, not being defeated or paralyzed by the mere fact of ambiguity.

Jane Flax challenges feminists to accept ambiguity and forego the delusions of "the longest lie," the belief that someone or something can save us from the risk of judgment and action.

> We need to learn ways of making claims about and acting upon injustice without transcendental guarantees or illusions of innocence. One of the dangerous consequences of transcendental notions of justice or knowledge is that they release us as discrete persons from full responsibility for our acts. We remain children, waiting, if our own powers fail, for the higher authorities to save us from the consequences of our actions. Such wishes depend on and express our complicity with what Nietzsche calls the "longest lie," the belief that "outside the haphazard and perilous experiments we perform there lies something (God, Science, Knowledge, Rationality, or Truth) which will, if only we perform the correct rituals, step in to save us."[16]

We can accept failure without a sense of humility, shame, or self-abnegation. We act, rather, in light of a basic recognition that we all make errors of judgment, we all find ourselves driven by pettiness, jealousy, and power. To be called on those failings by other people is not a sign of fundamental flaw or weakness, but is simply part of life. We need each other to be moral: we need clowns who can help puncture our pretensions; we need people to tell us when we have done damage; and we need to do the same for others.[17]

Contrast this logic of acting in the face of ambiguity with dualistic logic. The logic of racism, the logic of sexism, the logic of dualism is simple. I am not a woman, I am not black, I am not the despised or pitied other. I am not weak, overly emotional, hysterical, lax, stupid, sexually promiscuous. The logic of the prophet, the logic of the revolutionary vanguard, the logic of the progressive social critic, are all the same. I am not a fascist, I am not an oppressor. I am not abusive, controlling, rigid, self-righteous, narrow, self-interested, and determined to protect my own turf.

Although the political perspectives of each sensibility are ostensibly diametrically opposed, the attitude toward otherness and identity is the same. In each case the devalued, despised, or pitied Others are seen as fundamentally unlike us, as forces to be controlled, educated, defeated—either assimilated or destroyed. We are not them, and the world would be a better place without them. The world functions only by controlling them, keeping them in their place, even honoring them in their place (e.g., the paternalistic logic of protecting women, children, the masses).

Multicultural education offers another way of seeing identity and difference. The fundamental move is simple: I *could* be that; we *are* like the devalued and despised others. The fulcrum of moral evaluation and responsibility shifts, no longer predicated upon erecting barriers, ways of proving that we are not like "Them." The fulcrum of moral judgment and responsibility is the acknowledgment that we *are* Them, we are capable of being fascist, of being petty, tyrannical, lazy, weak, cruel, exploitative, and self-centered. And yet, here is the key difference, this recognition does not lead to shame or to humility. This recognition is perversely liberating. Over all, compassion. Over all, laughter.

This style of living with ambiguity is not a counterfactual ideal, but is given rich expression in the blues. We can hear in the blues a way of living with defeat and pain without succumbing to either cynicism or self-pity. What is the story of the blues? It is the wisdom of living with pain, a wisdom expressed by the novelist Simone Schwarz-Bart in *The Bridge of Beyond*. In this novel, we find a grandmother loving her granddaughter and teaching her what it takes to live well. This is not a story of defeating evil, of achieving a resolution of life's problems even for a generation, much less a resolution for all times. Rather, it is a way of living and of defying racism, sexism, and class exploitation, grounded in deep love and joy. The grandmother speaks of her love for her granddaughter with appreciation for the infinite wonder of life: "Ah, Telumee, my little crystal glass! What do you have that makes this old heart sing?"[18] Simone Schwarz-Bart also describes how to live with suffering. The mood here is neither fatalistic nor triumphant. The lesson about adversity, however, is succinct and clear: "Suffering is like a horse, and you must ride the horse and not let the horse ride you."[19]

The blues is the music of "riding the horse of suffering and not letting the horse ride you." As Ralph Ellison claims, the sensibility of the blues is not tragic, but tragi-comic.[20] And, according to Early, the blues provides a form of remembering the past without either sentiment or regret. The pain of the past is held, seen, felt, and noted, but not evaded through nostalgia; it is "a music of remembrance without being a music of the romance of remembrance, a music of the sentiment of remembrance.... [The] Blues is not a music of regret, a Wordsworthian quest for lost innocence."[21]

Ralph Ellison claims that the blues represents a way of seeing loss and dignity without evasion or sentiment, and writes of Bessie Smith, whose singing had this ritual power:

> Bessie Smith might have been a "blues queen" to the society at large, but within the tighter Negro community where the blues were part of a total way of life, and a major expression of an attitude toward life, she was a priestess, a celebrant who affirmed the values of the group and man's ability to deal with chaos.[22]

What is the role of ethics, of morality in dealing with chaos? I must first confess: I cringe at the sound of "ethics" and "morality," so redolent of judgment and self-satisfaction, of contempt and distrust of other people, so certain of having formulae for life's challenges, in short, so dishonest, so self-deluding, so unethical. There are other words that evoke similar reactions of distaste: peace, consensus, power-with, all these words of reason, calm, and harmony. Say them loudly and hear Kumbaya ringing through the air.

There are words I do like: passion, desire, outrage, audacity, justice, energy, fear, and, in case we start taking ourselves too seriously and slip into mighty-warrior land, kindness, gentleness, a willingness to risk hurt and failure, humor, and laughter.

What adds meaning, joy, and dimension to life? In addition to our work, our political involvements, what is the source of vitality and energy that sustains commitment, that provides the depth of engagement that can withstand rigorous, to-the-bone self-critique and transformation? The latter two capacities are often incompatible, those most committed to a cause or vision the most certain and closed to fundamental critique; those most open to critique and revisions the least certain about ethical standards, political strategies, and social analyses.

What compels compassion, self-criticism, and commitment? The power and draw of religion lies in the collective support of meaning and commitment. As a true believer, whether Christian, Jewish, Muslim, or any other, one has the comfort of belonging to something much larger than oneself. One is part of a community that is not merely a haphazard gathering of people but one belongs to a community that provides answers to the central questions of life. People belong to a religious group because there is a sense of being part of a collective with a means of helping us live as well as possible in the face of life's joys and challenges. Theology or doctrine provides a conceptual grasp of how religion makes sense of life, and ritual provides the embodiment of that sense, rituals of prayer, meditation, dance, and music. A powerful ritual is one in which people feel connected to something larger than themselves that provides meaning, direction, and grounding. The emotions that accompany this connection vary widely, from a quiet sense of contentment and security, to intense love, deep sorrow and release, the thrill of being challenged to be your best self, using all of your strengths and talents, feeling forgiven and accepted, experiencing ecstatic waves of energy and joy.

What I have described, the solace and challenge of belonging to a community, the joy and challenge of finding purpose in life, may seem unambiguously good. And, quite often, the emotional satisfaction and the direction for energy given by belonging to a religious community is taken as self-validating. Belonging feels so good, and the energies released for purposeful action so formidable, that surely the community's understanding of its task must be right and just.

Nothing could be further from the truth. Religious experience, while most certainly real and compelling, is fundamentally amoral. Belonging to a religious group, feeling connected to other people and to the sacred, can as easily fuel campaigns of genocide and coercion as movements of compassion and social transformation. Slave owners and abolitionists, participants in the Civil Rights movement and members of the Ku Klux Klan, alike drew comfort and challenge from their religious beliefs and their participation in religious communities.[23]

If religion, if belonging to a community larger than oneself, is both essential and amoral, where do we turn for critique and vision? One response to the pretensions of religion and morality is anti-ethics or antimorality. But hasn't that been done before? What was that fellows' name? You know, rhymes with "peachy"? (Although I doubt such an adjective was ever ascribed to him, except in sophomoric epics.)[24] I find it much too boring to stay in the mode of anti-ethics, too caught in mere reaction, and thus continuing to reify a structure and a discourse I find tedious and uninspiring. My focus here is, rather, positive: formulating a discourse in place of ethics, a postmodern alternative to ethics and morality, a sensibility of energy and passion, critique and construction, hope, persistence, laughter, and joy. Is it possible to hold together a recognition of the power and value of spirituality without denying its intrinsic dangers? To do so requires developing an ironic spirituality, one fueled by audacity and an appreciation of the perverse contradictions of life.[25]

This perspective is an alternative to an ethic of care and a postmodern ethic of responsibility as proposed by Zygmunt Bauman. The ethic of care too often downplays the costs and conflicts of relationships; Bauman's postmodern ethic misses the joy and reciprocity of care and downplays the paternalistic abuse endemic to asymmetrical relationships. Bauman grounds his postmodern ethics in the absolute claim of the Other, an Other who is "weak, vulnerable and without power."[26] Bauman acknowledges the costs and dangers of caring for others and, ironically, fails to acknowledge what could provide a check to the "genuine aporia of moral proximity," the joy of interacting with others in ways that are mutually supportive and challenging.[27]

Bauman's Other, following his interpretation of Levinas's description of "the Face," is devoid of agency, incapable of mutuality and reciprocity.

> The Other has no right to demand.... If she did voice her demands, she would just be invoking and enacting rights and obligations, norms and rules (so that we can go both to the court and litigate) or flexing her muscle (so that we can fight). But neither lawsuit nor fisticuffs are likely to placate a demand which stays stubbornly silent where the conventions are voluble and

vociferous. It is precisely the radicality arising from the unspo-
kenness that makes the demand rock-hard, indestructible,
unconditional—just the foundation on which the moral self
may rest its insecure security, its uncertain certainty. . . .

No harmonious ethics can be erected on this site—only the
straggly shoots of the never ending, never resolved moral anxiety will on this soil grow profusely. . . . And yet it is moral *anxiety*
that provides the only substance the moral self could ever
have. . . . *The moral self is a self always haunted by the suspicion that
it is not moral enough.*[28]

Bauman's description of this relationship is telling; the Other,
always female, has power and authority only as she remains passive.

Now I am truly a hostage (to merciless, insatiable pretensions of
the Other and her interminable fretting). If in the state of proximity the Other was the *authority* which grounded my responsibility . . . now she becomes a *force,* a resistance; The frailty of the
Other aroused the moral self in me; her forcefulness and mili-
tancy, on the other hand, cast me on the battle ground and keep
me there.[29]

Bauman goes so far as to deprive the Other of self-knowledge, and
casts his own forceful interpretation of her needs as being unmarked
by egotism or possessiveness:

Am I not a better judge of what is good for her? The Other may
fail to recognize herself in the interpretation; if she stays silent,
as inside the moral relationship she would, I will have no means
to learn of the disagreement; if she breaks the silence, acquires a
voice of her own provoked by the sound of my voice, and so
begins to resist, it is now her self-reading against my reading-
for-her; and if I want to make sure that my responsibility has
been exercised in full. . . I will feel obliged to include in my
responsibility also the duty to overcome what I can see as nothing else but her ignorance, or *mis*-interpretation, of "her own
best interest.". . .

This is the genuine aporia of moral proximity. . . .

Because I am responsible . . . I must force the other to submit
to what I, in my best conscience, interpret as "her own good."

> There is no point in accusing me of greed or possessiveness, even of egotism: I still act *for the Other's sake,* I am still a moral self, unconcerned with self-interest, not counting my costs, ready for sacrifice. There is but a thin line between care and oppression.[30]

Bauman is dangerously wrong in his vision of asymmetrical reciprocity and care. He casts responsibility as an absolute burden, missing thereby the rewards of caring and the checks that come to our manipulation of others "for their own good."[31] We care for others because it gives us joy. By recognizing this, we can guard against two forms of exploitation and manipulation: us controlling others, maintaining their dependence on us because it gives us pleasure; or giving in ways that do not bring joy, that do not seem a vital expression of our creativity and strength, but are rather us being used by another.

I do not want to frame this alternative spiral of interpretation in terms of an ethic of care. As currently formulated, the ethic of care seems to derive from women's powerlessness and not from our insights and strength. Think about the virtues attributed to women— the focus on nurturing, on making sure that no one is hurt.[32]

There can be a form of moral reasoning that seeks to take into account the impact of our actions on all concerned. It is dangerous, however, if we assume that we can balance all needs, that we can insure that there will be no harm, or at least no undue harm. This view downplays the degree of conflict at work in human relations and in connection with nature. This same concern that no one be hurt can reflect the fear of conflict and the fear of being attacked, criticized, and rejected.

To criticize this stance—the hope that no one will be hurt—can seem heartless. It is important to understand why many white, relatively privileged women are afraid of conflict. Our identities are based on relationships. Until the 1970s, women did not have equal access to education, employment, or credit. Our livelihoods were often dependent on pleasing men, those who supported us financially as husbands or fathers, those who were our employers.[33] The economic dependence on men was compounded by fear of violence from those same men. There were no shelters for battered women, little recourse in the courts, little help from police officers, even from family, friends, and church. Women were often told to return to their husbands even after severe beatings.[34]

Little wonder, then, that we learned to fear conflict. Little wonder, then, that we wanted to make sure that no one was hurt. Conflict with men could mean the loss of economic security and physical attack; conflict with other women could mean losing one's place in a supportive circle of friends. Why not the same fear of conflict for black women? Is it because there were fewer rewards for compliance for black women? Many black women learned other ways of surviving in the face of violence and economic discrimination, ways that have provided sustenance for black communities, and yet have their own costs.[35]

As white women gained power, however, the habits we learned to survive no longer served us. Ironically, though rooted in our marginalization, these habits have become the vehicle of maintaining control and privilege—i.e., silencing differences among women in regard to race and ideology, differences we need to maintain community and coalitions. White women need an ethic of conflict.[36] We can learn from womanists how to work with our conflicts, not crumble in the face of them, avoid them at all costs, or exclude those people seen as the source of conflicts.

What does it mean to think of human vitality in light of the experiences of women? Many women know the costs and dangers of care, the costs and dangers of allowing ourselves to be defined by meeting the needs of others. We know as well the joy, the larger sense of self that comes from defining ourselves in relationship to others—a relationship more like that described by Buber than by Bauman; a relationship that incorporates respect as well as care; a relationship that includes being cared for, being seen, being recognized by the ones for whom we feel care.[37] Levinas's description of abnegation in the face of the other, oddly enough taken up by Bauman in his postmodern ethos, is a denial of the joy of being cared for, of being seen, a denial of the mutuality that is part of relationships.

My aim is to provide a tonic: when it is no longer possible to be self-righteous, even in our caring, let us try to be decent. What can we call this perspective? Decentism? Decentism . . . I like that as a name: clear, to the point, and much too homely to cover any grand causes or legitimize the leadership of any vanguard.

Contrast this position with Bauman's rejection of "decency" as an adequate moral standard:

> I have been chosen by this responsibility which I bear alone—and thus my standards cannot be ordinary, statistically average, or commonly shared. The saints are *unique* people, people who do things other people shirk—being too afraid, or too weak, or too selfish to do them—and things which one would not in good conscience demand that they do, since doing them goes beyond and above "sheer decency" or "the call of duty."[38]

With Bauman's aspiration to a postmodern saintliness, we skirt, as he acknowledges, the "thin line between care and oppression."[39] With the ethos of style and decency, we face other risks. We may easily fall from concern and responsibility to indifference and callousness. The break, the shock, the jolt, the gift that brings us back from cavalier indifference is not Bauman's weak and vulnerable Other, but the dignity, voice, presence and *demand* of others, other people calling us to accountability, other people inviting us to interactions fraught with risk and joy.

What is the foundation of moral action, of individuals and groups acting with courage, insight, and vision to end some form of systemic injustice? There is none. Bauman is right: there are no rules, no principles, no authorities that can insure either individuals or collectives acting in responsible ways (e.g., not cheating, polluting, exploiting others for personal gain as part of their/our daily lives).[40] There are no principles, no rules, no authorities that can insure that genocide will be stopped, that the abuse of children will end, that men will stop raping and exploiting women. Principles can be voided by counterprinciples, (e.g., social order transcends individual freedom). Rules are swept aside by emotions, by fear, and by shortsightedness.

And yet, at times, people are decent. At times, grave forms of injustice are challenged and even eradicated. Some people do find their life work in building and sustaining creativity and respect: nurses and doctors giving considerate care, teachers challenging and respecting students.[41] Some employers pay their workers fairly and encourage participation, job safety, and environmental responsibility. Injustice is challenged: child labor laws are enforced; some people and governments resisted the Holocaust; apartheid was overthrown and a new social order is in the process of being built.

All these forms of individual and collective daily decency, all these forms of systemic transformation are, of course, partial. There is no perfect justice. All are, of course, limited in scope and fragile. They can be undone.

Working on issues of identity, of justice, of homelessness, of the oppression of women, is extremely urgent, serious, worthy of the best of our time and attention, and quite literally a matter of life and death for many people. And yet it is perversely, perhaps, easier to respond to such problems when seen as part of the ongoing framework of being human and not as an unprecedented crisis in the history of humankind. Morris Miller raises this suggestion in regard to our current economic "crisis":

> In times of stress, when profound structural change seems imminent, the air fills with messages salted on one side with a trace of panic and sweetened on the other with escapist unrealizable options. (Where do you run when the sky is falling? Jonestown?)[42]

At times, we act with courage and compassion. We take risks, we learn from our mistakes, we respond appropriately to the needs of others. The alternative to fanaticism is simple: gratitude for joy and pleasure, mourning, rage, and resilience in the face of life's horrors. The mystery of human evil lies in peoples' attempts to hold on to the fragile gift of goodness; we try to make it binding, eternal, and absolute.

What is the wellspring of decency? What is the wellspring of courage, transformation, and persistence? Acts of respect, of courage, of resistance and transformation spring from a deep reservoir of vitality and joy: joy in living fully and well, joy in breathing, walking, running, dancing, making love. The joy of touch, smell, and taste; the joy of music that soars, laughing, raging, desiring, delighting, exalting in the wonder of life; the joy of thinking, of understanding connections, drawing together disparate pieces of information; the joy of seeing, analyzing, and strategizing; even the delight of "lowly beginnings."

The sensibility I invoke could be traced through Foucault to Nietzsche. Foucault suggested that we follow Nietzsche and look at the history (what he calls the genealogy) of our philosophies, political projects, and institutions with an eye to the ways in which "beginnings are lowly."

> History also teaches how to laugh at the solemnities of the origin. The lofty origin is no more than "a metaphysical extension which arises from the belief that things are most precious and essential at the moment of birth." We tend to think that this is the moment of their greatest perfection, when they emerged dazzling from the hands of a creator or in the shadowless light of a first morning. The origin always precedes the Fall.... But historical beginnings are lowly: not in the sense of modest or discreet like the steps of a dove, but derisive and ironic, capable of undoing every infatuation."[43]

I may be giving this a Texas spin. Whenever I think of lowly beginnings, I do not feel outrage or despair, but rather, find it all quite amusing. To cite Molly Ivins,

> I love America, in part because, as Marianne Moore once wrote in another context, "It is an honor to witness so much confusion." Ted Morgan is an American who was born a French aristocrat. One reason he decided to become an American is because he so enjoys watching our countrymen confronted with a problem. Me too. We immediately mount horse and charge off in 360 different directions....
>
> It is not the symphony of voices in sweet concert I enjoy, but the cacophony of democracy, the brouhahas and the donnybrooks, the full-throated roar of a free people busy using their right to freedom of speech. Democracy requires rather a large

tolerance for confusion and a secret relish for dissent. This is not a good country for those who are fond of unanimity and uniformity.[44]

What does it take to enjoy the "cacophony of democracy, the brouhahas and donnybrooks"? Maybe Molly Ivins is right in her explanation of the optimism and perverse sense of taking on the world while laughing at ourselves so characteristic of many Texans: there is lithium in the drinking water.[45] A factor that I, for one, do not discount, knowing full well the culture of a grandmother who, in responding to one of my sophomoric (literally) declarations that everything was corrupt and I was utterly hopeless about the possibility of social change, just laughed, shook her head, and said, "Well, I guess you can look at life like that if you want to." Powerfully unsaid was the corollary question, "But child, why would anyone want to?"

Why would anyone want to give up on life? Fear, abuse, being beaten down again and again. Sometimes we lose. Our love of life can be destroyed, yet our love of life can also be nourished by the healing waters of rage, compassion, and respect. Justice, compassion, decency, all well up from deep reservoirs of respect: respect for the rhythms of life, the realization that there is nothing profane, nothing contemptible in our bodiliness; thus respect even of death and decay; respect even of pain. The wellspring of insight and persistence is also rage: rage at that which violates unnecessarily the rhythms of life.

There is another dimension of the wellspring of moral action, not just acceptance of the limits of life, but feeling fully the limits and boundaries of life. We grieve because of death. It is not easy when those we love suffer and die. Yet the horizon, the shape, the shading of our love is that we love people who will die.

The wellspring of decency is loving this life in which people die, people suffer, there are limits, and we make mistakes.[46] The wellspring, then, of moral action is not utopia, not a counterfactual vision, not a declaration that the world could and should be otherwise. Rather, it is a deep affirmation of the joy, richness, and blessing that the world is. The ground of challenging exploitation, injustice, and oppression is not a vision of how the world could be or will be in the future in the reign of God, or after the revolution. The ground of challenging injustice is gratitude, the heartfelt desire to honor the wonder of that which is; to cherish, to celebrate, to delight in the many gifts and joys of life.

Notes

PREFACE

1. Michael Lerner, *The Politics of Meaning: Restoring Hope and Possibility in an Age of Cynicism* (Reading, MA: Addison-Wesley, 1996).

2. Carol Lee Sanchez, conversation, April 1993.

3. Rosabeth Moss Kanter, *Men and Women of the Corporation* (New York: Basic Books, 1977).

4. Jacob Heilbrunn, "Neocon vs. Theocon," *The New Republic* (December 30, 1996), p. 22.

5. The distinction between power-over and power-with was first developed by Mary Parker Follett and has been used by feminists to differentiate between coercive power, in which power is exercised other others, and enabling power, in which the exercise of power evokes in others the ability to act creatively and independently. For a thorough discussion of power-with and its use in education, see Seth Kreisberg, *Transforming Power: Domination, Empowerment and Education* (Albany, NY: State University of New York, 1992).

6. bell hooks, "Feminism and Racism: The Struggle Continues," *Z Magazine*, (July/August 1990), p. 41.

7. Michael Lerner, *Surplus Powerlessness: The Psychodynamics of Everyday Life and the Psychology of Individual and Social Transformation* (Atlantic Highlands, NJ: Humanities Press International, 1991), ch. 14.

8. Ann Douglas, *Terrible Honesty: Mongrel Manhattan in the 1920s* (New York: Farrar, Straus and Giroux, 1995), p. 3.

9. Malcolm X, *The Autobiography of Malcolm X as told to Alex Haley* (New York: Ballantine Books, 1964), p. 281.

10. The American dream of increasing prosperity is true for only a small proportion of the American population. Peter Passell reports on the well-known trends

in the American economy: between 1973 and 1993 "the gap between the top and the bottom widened sharply. An American at the 10th percentile of the economic pecking order suffered a 21 percent decline in income, while an American in the 90th percentile enjoyed a 22 percent gain." Peter Passell, "The rich are getting richer, etc., and it's likely to remain that way." *New York Times*, March 28, 1996, p. C2. Derrick Bell claims that salaries of top executives increased by 220 percent from 1977 to 1990. "Had the nation's manufacturing workers shared in the productivity gains and profits to the same extent as management, the average factory laborer today would be earning more than $81,000 per year." Derrick Bell, *Gospel Choirs: Psalms of Survival in an Alien Land Called Home* (New York: Basic Books, 1996), p. 7.

   11. Theophus H. Smith, *Conjuring Culture: Biblical Formations of Black America* (New York: Oxford University Press, 1994).

   12. Immanual Kant, *Fundamental Principles of the Metaphysics of Morals,* trans. T. K. Abbott (Buffalo, NY: Prometheus, 1987), p. 31.

CHAPTER 1

   1. Patricia Williams, *The Alchemy of Race and Rights: Diary of a Law Professor* (Cambridge: Harvard University Press, 1991).

   2. Derrick Bell summarizes the goals of each of his previous works in *Gospel Choirs: Psalms of Survival in an Alien Land Called Home* (New York: Basic Books, 1996), p. 12.

   3. Ibid.

   4. Ibid.

   5. Garth Kasimu Baker-Fletcher, *XODUS: An African American Male Journey* (Minneapolis: Fortress Press, 1995). Peter McLaren describes a similar longing in "Introduction: Fashioning *Los Olvidados* in the Age of Cynical Reason," in *Revolutionary Multiculturalism: Pedagogies of Dissent for the New Millennium* (Boulder, CO: Westview, 1997).

   6. Eleanor Wilner, "Those Who Come After," in *Otherwise* (Chicago: University of Chicago Press, 1993), pp. 91–92.

   7. Ibid., p. 92.

   8. Charles Krauthammer, "The End of Heroism," *Time* (February 10, 1997), p. 88.

   9. Stephen Jay Gould, *Wonderful Life: The Burgess Shale and the Nature of History* (New York: W.W. Norton, 1989), p. 25.

   10. Ibid., p. 48.

   11. Ibid., p. 44.

   12. James Gleick, *Chaos: Making a New* Science (New York: Penguin, 1987) p. 3 as cited by Andrew W. Hayes, "An Introduction to Chaos and Law," *UMKC Law Review* 60, 4 (1992): 759.

   13. Hayes, "An Introduction," p. 760.

14. Ibid., p. 762.

15. Ibid., p. 766.

16. Ibid.

17. Molly Ivins, *Nothin' But Good Times Ahead* (New York: Vintage, 1994), p. xi.

18. Gould, *Wonderful Life,* pp. 155–57.

19. Ibid., p. 291.

20. Michel Foucault, "The Political Technology of Individuals," in *Technologies of the Self,* edited by Luther H. Martin, Huck Gutman, and Patrick H. Hutton (Amherst, MA: University of Massachusetts, 1988), p. 146.

21. Michel Foucault, *Discipline and Punish: The Birth of the Prison,* trans. Alan Sheridan (New York: Random House, 1977), pp. 16, 235, 297, as cited by James Miller, *The Passion of Michel Foucault* (New York: Doubleday, 1993), p. 212.

22. Michel Foucault, "Revolutionary Action: 'Until Now'," in *Language, Counter-memory, Practice: Selected Essays and Interviews by Michel Foucault,* ed. and with an introduction by Donald F. Bouchard (Ithaca, NY: Cornell University Press, 1977), pp. 212–22.

23. Michel Foucault, "Space Knowledge and Power," *The Foucault Reader,* ed. Paul Rabinow (New York: Pantheon, 1984), p. 249.

24. Ibid.

25. See for example, Foucault's analysis of a specific instance of oppression: the imprisonment of political dissidents in the Soviet Union, and the theories that avoid addressing the meaning and function of that event. Michel Foucault, "Powers and Strategies," in *Power/Knowledge: Selected Interviews and Other Writings, 1972–1977* (New York: Pantheon, 1980), pp. 134–45.

26. Miller, *The Passion of Foucault,* p. 384.

27. My alternative to Foucault's politics may be understood as a type of utilitarianism, but one that acknowledges the appropriateness of Foucault's utilization of Benthams' Panopticon as a model of domination. It may also be seen as a type of pragmatism, but one that incorporates Cornel West's and Rebecca Chopp's critique of pragmatism's tendency to elide the depth of injustice and the costs and chaos of social transformation. Rebecca Chopp, "Feminism's Theological Pragmatics: A Social Naturalism of Women's Experience," in *Journal of Religion,* April 1987 (Volume 67, number 2), pp. 239–56; Cornel West, *The American Evasion of Philosophy: A Genealogy of Pragmatism* (Madison, WI: University of Wisconsin Press, 1989).

28. While much of James Miller's analysis of Foucault's thought is insightful, I find that he misses the ambiguity in Foucault's discussion of transgression and political violence. Foucault was fascinated by the ambiguity of transgression. At times he extols its violence: "It [transgression] serves as a glorification of the nature it excludes: the limit opens violently onto the limitless, finds itself suddenly carried away by the content it had rejected and fulfilled by this alien plenitude which invades it to the core of its being.... And yet, toward what is transgression unleashed in its movement of

pure violence, if not that which imprisons it; toward the limit and those elements it contains? (pp. 34–35) In the same essay, however, Foucault insists that transgression has nothing to do with the scandalous or subversive: "Transgression is neither violence in a divided world (in an ethical world) nor a victory over limits (in a dialectical or revolutionary world): and exactly for this reason, its role is to measure the excessive distance that it opens at the heart of the limit and to trace the flashing line that causes the limit to arise. Transgression contains nothing negative, but it affirms limited being...." (p. 35). Transgression "may designate the existence of difference" (p. 36). Michel Foucault, "A Preface to Transgression," in *Language, Counter-memory, Practice.*

29. Michel Foucault, "Conversazione con Michel Foucault," *La fiera letteraria,* 39, September 28, 1967, as translated and cited by Miller, p. 173.

30. Miller, p. 173.

31. Ibid., p. 206.

32. See for example, the following works. Foucault analyzed the memoirs of a man convicted of murder in *I, Pierre Riviere, having slaughtered my mother, my sister and my brother...,* trans. Frank Jellinek (New York: Pantheon, 1975). He affirms the need for vengeance and retribution, and uses the September massacres of 1792 as an "approximation to act of popular justice." "On Popular Justice: A Discussion with Maoists," in *Power/Knowledge: Selected Interviews and Other Writings, 1972–1977,* ed. Colin Gordon (New York: Pantheon, 1980), pp. 1, 8, 28, 29. He often affirmed the necessity of sacrifice: see the following two essays from *Language, Counter-memory, Practice:* "What is an Author?" and "Nietzsche, Genealogy and History." He advocated a philosophy that in contrast to "good sense" gives "free rein" to "ill will and ill humor." ("Theatrum Philosophicum," in *Language, Counter-memory, Practice,* pp. 182, 191.) He interpreted history as the repeated play of domination and violence. ("Nietzsche, Genealogy and History," in *Language, Counter-memory, Practice,* pp. 150–151.)

33. Miller, pp. 206–07.

34. Ibid., pp. 166–67.

35. Ibid., p. 236.

36. Ibid., pp. 237–38.

37. Ibid., p. 238.

38. Ibid., p. 239.

39. Ibid., pp. 238–39.

40. Michel Foucault, "Creation d'un groupe d'information sur les prisons," *Esprit,* 3 (March 1971) p. 532 as cited by Miller, p. 189.

41. Foucault, "Revolutionary Action 'Until Now'," p. 227.

42. Miller, p. 235.

43. Michel Foucault, "Preface," to Deleuze and Guattari, *Anti-Oedipus,* p. xiii, as cited by Miller, p. 240.

44. Foucault, "Revolutionary Action," p. 231.

45. Miller, pp. 312–13.

46. Ibid., p. 327.

47. Michel Foucault, "Talk with Philosophers 23 October 1980" tape filed in the Centre Michel Foucault and transcribed by James Miller, cited by Miller, p. 342.

48. Miller, p. 165.

49. Rather than examining jazz, one could also turn to gospel music, as do James Cone and Derrick Bell. In *Gospel Choirs,* Bell celebrates the power of gospel music: "Either in the music itself, or in the determination to keep going, sparked and nurtured by the music, we must learn to do what our enslaved ancestors did. We do have resources" (p. 15). Mahalia Jackson, in an interview with George Simon, clearly stated her reasons for preferring gospel to jazz, despite their similarities. "Good jazz has to have a soul and feeling, like the blues.... I sing Divine songs and they have more to offer than jazz does.... Another thing about jazz—it makes people happy on the surface, but when it's over, it's through. But a Gospel song lasts—it penetrates much deeper and stays with you." George T. Simon, "Mahalia Jackson," in *Reading Jazz: A Gathering of Autobiography, Reportage and Criticism from 1919 to Now,* ed. Robert Gottlieb (New York: Pantheon, 1996), p. 633. The factor that led Mahalia Jackson to prefer gospel is the characteristic that leads me to prefer jazz: its power is in its crystallization of the present.

50. Jed Rasula, "The Media of Memory: The Seductive Menace of Records in Jazz History," in *Jazz Among the Discourses,* ed. Krin Gabbard (Durham, NC: Duke University Press, 1995), p. 152.

51. Toni Cade Bambara, *The Salt Eaters* (New York: Vintage, 1981).

52. Theophus Smith, *Conjuring Culture: Biblical Formations of Black America* (New York: Oxford University Press, 1994), p. 123.

53. Ibid.

54. Ibid.

55. Gerald Early, *Tuxedo Junction: Essays on American Culture* (New York: Ecco, 1992), p. 263.

56. Ibid.

57. Ralph Ellison, *Shadow and Act* (London: Secker and Warburg, 1964), pp. 189–90.

58. Neil Leonard, *Jazz: Myth and Religion* (New York: Oxford University Press, 1987), p. 58.

59. See the fuller discourse on the conjuction of racism, jazz, and American and African American identity in Amiri Baraka and Amina Baraka, *The Music: Reflections on Jazz and Blues* (New York: William Morrow, 1987), pp. 191, 265; Ann Douglas, *Terrible Honesty: Mongrel Manhattan in the 1920s* (New York: Farrar, Straus and Giroux, 1995), pp. 74–116, and the following essays, all in *Jazz Among the Discourses,* ed. Krin Gabbard (Durham: Duke University Press, 1995); Bernard Gendron, "Moldy Figs and Modernists: Jazz at War (1942–1946)," pp. 31–56; Steven B. Elworth, "Jazz in Crisis, 1948–1958: Ideology and Representation," pp. 57–75; Eric Lott, "Double V, Double-Time: Bebop's Politics of Style," pp. 256–74.

60. Elworth, "Jazz in Crisis," Krin Gabbard, "Introduction: The Jazz Canon and its Consequences," pp. 1–30, William Howland Kenney, "Historical Context and the Definition of Jazz: Putting More of the History in 'Jazz History'," pp. 100–116, in Gabbard, *Jazz Among the Discourses*.

61. Krin Gabbard, "Introduction: Writing the Other History," in *Representing Jazz*, ed. Krin Gabbard (Durham, NC: Duke University Press, 1995), p. 2.

62. Bernard Holland, "A Wagnerian Legacy of Beauty and Unease," *New York Times* (March 27, 1997), pp. B-1, B-7.

63. Ibid., p. B-7.

64. Ibid.

65. Ibid.

66. Robert Walser, "Out of Notes: Signification, Interpretation and the Problem of Miles Davis," in Gabbard, *Jazz Among the Discourses*, p. 165.

67. James Collier, *Jazz: The American Theme Song* (New York: Oxford University Press, 1993), p. 52.

68. Amiri Baraka and Amina Baraka, *The Music*, p. 24.

69. Lott, "Double V, Double-Time," p. 243.

70. Miller, "The Passion of Foucault," p. 340.

71. Niels-Henning Ørsted Pedersen, cited by Bob Blumenthal, liner notes for *A Tribute to Oscar Peterson, Live at the Town Hall*, Telarc, 1997.

72. Joel Siegel, liner notes, Billie Holiday, Polygram, 1991.

73. It is the acknowledgment of failure that most clearly separates my use of jazz and chaos theory from that of Wheatley and her use of chaos theory as a model for organizational growth. Wheatley claims that "the things we fear most in organizations—fluctuations, disturbances, imbalances—need not be signs of an impending disorder that will destroy us. Instead, fluctuations are the primary sources of creativity" (p. 207). Wheatley refers to jazz as a metaphor for leadership, yet highlights only the creativity. She speaks of escaping fear, and evokes the image of "ancient Gaia" (p. 23) who "always pull[s] forth order" (p. 137). Margaret J. Wheatley, *Leadership and the New Science: Learning about Organization from an Orderly Universe* (San Francisco: Berrett-Koehler, 1994).

74. Jeff Rosen, liner notes, *Miles and Coltrane*, Columbia, 1973.

75. Benny Green, "Billie Holiday," cited in *Reading Jazz: A Gathering of Autobiography, Reportage, and Criticism from 1919 to Now*, ed. Robert Gottlieb (New York: Pantheon, 1996), p. 942.

76. Humphrey Littleton, "Bessie Smith," in Gottlieb, *Reading Jazz*, p. 927.

77. Bill Evans, cited by Gene Less, "The Poet: Bill Evans," in Gottlieb, *Reading Jazz*, p. 419.

78. Sidney Bechet, "Sidney Bechet," in Gottlieb, *Reading Jazz*, p. 13.

79. Miles Davis, "Miles Davis," in Gottlieb, *Reading Jazz*, pp. 242–43.

80. Art Blakey, "Art Blakey," in Gottlieb, *Reading Jazz*, p. 208.

81.   Wynton Marsalis, quoted by Peter Watrous, "Veteran Saxophonists Show More Than Age," *New York Times* (April 15, 1996), p. B-3.

82.   Edwards, quoted by Watrous, "Veteran Saxophonists," p. B-5.

83.   Neil Tesser, interview of Chico Freeman for the liner notes for *Chico Freeman Quintet Featuring Arthur Blythe,* Contemporary Records, 1995.

84.   Jon Poses, liner notes for *Turn Around: Joanne Brackeen,* Evidence, 1995.

CHAPTER 2

1.   For indices of women's power worldwide as measured by percentages of legislators, literacy, mortality rates, and participation in the workforce, see Barbara Nelson and Najma Chowdhury, eds., *Women and Politics Worldwide* (New Haven: Yale University Press, 1994).

2.   See the critique of dualism in Rosemary Radford Ruether, *Sexism and God-Talk: Toward a Feminist Theology* (Boston: Beacon, 1983); Hyun Kyung Chung, *Struggle to Be the Sun Again: Introducing Asian Women's Theology* (Maryknoll, NY: Orbis, 1990); Judith Plaskow, *Standing Again at Sinai: Judaism from a Feminist Perspective* (San Francisco: Harper & Row, 1990); Emilie M. Townes, ed., *A Troubling in My Soul: Womanist Perspective on Evil and Suffering* (Maryknoll, NY: Orbis Books, 1993); Ada María Isasi-Díaz, *Mujerista Theology: A Theology for the Twenty-First Century* (Maryknoll, NY: Orbis, 1996); Kathleen M. Sands, *Escape From Paradise: Evil and Tragedy in Feminist Theology* (Minneapolis: Fortress, 1994); and Edward Farley, *Good and Evil: Interpreting a Human Condition* (Philadelphia: Fortress, 1991).

3.   There is a voluminous literature that explains the significance of the liberation of women. See, for example, Mary Daly, *Beyond God the Father: Toward a Philosophy of Women's Liberation* (Boston: Beacon, 1973); Beverly Wildung Harrison, *Making the Connections: Essays in Feminist Social Ethics,* ed. Carol S. Robb (Boston: Beacon, 1985); Beverly Wildung Harrison, *Our Right to Choose: Toward a New Ethic of Abortion* (Boston: Beacon, 1983); Nancy F. Cott, *The Grounding of Modern Feminism* (New Haven: Yale University Press, 1989); and Patricia Hill Collins, *Black Feminist Thought: Knowledge, Consciousness and the Politics of Empowerment* (New York: Routledge, 1991).

4.   See the discussion of these conflicts in Angela Y. Davis, *Women, Race and Class* (New York: Vintage, 1983); Papusa Molina, "Recognizing, Accepting and Celebrating Our Differences," in *Making Face, Making Soul,* ed. Gloria Anzaldua (San Francisco: Spinsters, 1990); Jane Flax, "The End of Innocence," in *Feminists Theorize the Political,* ed. Judith Butler and Joan W. Scott (New York: Routledge, 1992), p. 457.

5.   See Sarah Lucia Hoagland, *Lesbian Ethics: Toward New Value* (Palo Alto, CA: Institute of Lesbian Studies, 1988); Naomi Wolf, *Fire with Fire: The New Female Power and How to Use It* (New York: Fawcett Columbine, 1993); and Brigit P. C. McCallum, *Re-Worlding Toward Solidarity: Healing and Empowerment in the Feminist Spiritual Community,* dissertation (Cambridge, MA: Harvard University, July 1993).

6. Jane Mansbridge, *Why We Lost the ERA* (Chicago: University of Chicago Press, 1986); Susan Faludi, *Backlash: The Undeclared War Against American Women* (New York: Crown, 1991); Wolf, *Fire with Fire*; Sheila Rowbotham, *Hidden From History: Rediscovering Women in History from the Seventeenth Century to the Present* (New York: Putnam, 1973), and *The Past Is Before Us: Feminism in Action Since the 1960's* (Boston: Beacon, 1991); Linda Gordon, *Heroes of Their Own Lives: The Politics and History of Family Violence* (New York: Viking, 1988); Marie Fortune, *Sexual Violence: The Unmentionable Sin, An Ethical and Pastoral Perspective* (New York: Pilgrim, 1983).

7. See Ruether, *Sexism and God-Talk*; Rita Nakashima Brock, *Journeys by Heart: A Christology of Erotic Power* (New York: Crossroad, 1991); Fatima Mernissi, *The Veil and the Male Elite: A Feminist Interpretation of Women's Rights in Islam,* trans. of *Le Harem Politique* (Reading, MA: Addison-Wesley, 1991); Susanna Heschel, *On Being a Jewish Feminist* (New York: Schocken, 1983); Plaskow, *Standing Again at Sinai*; Elisabeth Schüssler Fiorenza, *In Memory of Her: A Feminist Theological Reconstruction of Christian Origins* (New York: Crossroad, 1983); Betty Deberg, *Ungodly Women: Gender and the First Wave of American Fundamentalism* (Minneapolis: Fortress, 1990).

8. See the following works for a thorough discussion of these critiques: Janet Jakobsen, *Working Alliances and the Politics of Difference: Diversity in Feminist Ethics* (Bloomington: Indiana University Press, forthcoming); Patricia Hill Collins, *Black Feminist Thought: Knowledge, Consciousness, and the Politics of Empowerment* (New York: Routledge, 1991); Gloria Anzaldua, "Haciendo Caras, Una Entrada," in *Making Face, Making Soul* (San Francisco: Spinsters, 1990); Janet Zandy, ed., *Calling Home: Working Class Women's Writings, An Anthology* (New Brunswick, NJ: Rutgers University Press, 1985); Angela Y. Davis, *Women, Race and Class* (New York: Vintage, 1983); bell hooks, *Ain't I a Woman: Black Women and Feminism* (Boston: South End, 1981); bell hooks, *Feminist Theory: From Margin to Center* (Boston: South End, 1984); bell hooks, *Talking Back: Thinking Feminist, Thinking Black* (Boston: South End, 1989); bell hooks, *Yearning: Race, Gender, Culture and Politics* (New York: South End, 1990); Cherrie Moraga and Gloria Anzaldua, eds., *This Bridge Called My Back: Writings by Radical Women of Color* (Watertown, MA: Persephone, 1981); Gloria Anzaldua, ed., *Making Face, Making Soul* (San Francisco: Spinsters, 1990); Katie Cannon, *Katie's Canon: Womanism and the Soul of the Black Community* (New York: Continuum, 1995), and *Black Womanist Ethics* (Atlanta, GA: Scholars Press, 1988).

9. See Elisabeth Spelman, *Inessential Woman: Problems of Exclusion in Feminist Thought* (Boston: Beacon, 1990); Sheila Greeve Davaney, "The Limits of the Appeal to Women's Experience," in *Shaping New Vision: Gender and Values in American Culture,* ed. C. W. Atkinson, C. H. Buchanan, and M. R. Miles (Ann Arbor, MI: UMI Research Press, 1987).

10. Nancy Fraser, *Justus Interruptus: Critical Reflections on the "Postsocialist" Condition* (New York: Routledge, 1997).

11. See, for example, Liza Fiol-Matta and Mariam K. Chamberland, eds., *Women of Color and the Multicultural Curriculum: Transforming the College Classroom* (New York: Feminist Press, 1994); Trinh T. Minh-ha, *Woman, Native, Other: Writing Postcoloniality and Feminism* (Bloomington: Indiana University Press, 1989); Davis, *Women, Race and Class*; Anzaldua, *Making Face, Making Soul*; Moraga and Anzaldua, *This Bridge Called My Back*.

12. See Molina, "Recognizing, Accepting"; Susan Thistlethewaite, *Sex, Race and God: Christian Feminism in Black and White* (New York: Crossroad, 1989); Ann Douglas, *Terrible Honesty: Mongel Manhattan in the 1920s* (New York: Farrar Straus Giroux, 1995); Ruth Frankenberg, *White Women, Race Matters: The Social Construction of Whiteness* (Minneapolis, MN: University of Minnesota Press, 1993); Janet Helms, *A Race Is a Nice Thing to Have: A Guide to Being a White Person or Understanding the White Person in Your Life* (Topeka, KS: Content Communications, 1992); Joan Steinau Lester, *The Future of White Men and Other Diversity Dilemmas* (Berkeley, CA: Conari, 1994).

13. Jane Flax, "The End of Innocence," in *Feminists Theorize the Political,* ed. Judith Butler and Joan W. Scott (New York: Routledge, 1992), pp. 445–63. For other criticisms of female innocence see Carol Christ, *Diving Deep and Surfacing: Woman Writers on Spiritual Quest* (Boston: Beacon, 1980); Rosemary Radford Ruether, *Gaia and God: An Ecofeminist Theology of Earth Healing* (San Francisco: Harper, 1993); Rita Nakashima Brock, *Journeys By Heart: A Christology of Erotic Power* (New York: Crossroad, 1991); Thistlethewaite, *Sex, Race and God*; Kathleen M. Sands, *Escape From Paradise: Evil and Tragedy in Feminist Theology* (Minneapolis, MN: Fortress, 1994).

14. Flax, "End of Innocence," p. 454.

15. Mary McClintock Fulkerson, *Changing the Subject: Women's Discourses and Feminist Theology* (Minneapolis, MN: Fortress, 1994).

16. Theophus Smith, *Conjuring Culture,* p. 5.

17. Ibid., p. 6.

18. Ibid.

19. Ibid., p. 56.

20. Ibid., p. 31.

21. Ibid., p. 43.

22. See Rosemary Radford Ruether, *Faith and Fratricide: The Theological Roots of Anti-Semitism* (New York: Seabury, 1974).

23. Gary Oxenhandler, "GroupThink & Self Awareness," unpublished essay (1992) p. 1; and Rosabeth Moss Kanter, *The Change Masters: Innovation and Entrepreneurship in the American Corporation* (New York: Simon and Schuster, 1983), p. 288.

24. Oxenhandler, "GroupThink," p. 3.

25. Irving L. Janus, cited by Oxenhandler, "GroupThink," p. 2.

26. Kanter, *The Change Masters,* p. 288.

27. Ibid., pp. 288–89.

28. Ibid., pp. 285–86.

29. Ibid., p. 285.

30. Ibid., p. 288.

31. Oxenhandler, "GroupThink," p. 5.

32. Clifford Geertz, *Local Knowledges: Further Essays in Anthropology* (New York: Basic Books, 1983), p. 146.

33. Maureen Dowd, "G.O.P.'s Rising Star Pledges to Right Wrongs of the Left," *New York Times*, pg. A1 (con't B3), November 10, 1994.

34. Smith, *Conjuring Culture,* p. 223.

35. Ruether, *Faith and Fratricide.*

36. For a thorough analysis and critique of the apocalyptic imagination, see Catherine Keller, *Apocalypse Now: A Feminist Guide to the End of the World* (Boston: Beacon Press, 1996). Keller also points to the dangers of the prophetic stance (p. 217) and advocates instead "radical relatedness" (p. 30). Although she does not explore the implications of jazz as an imaginative alternative to apocalypse, she does conclude her book with the image of jazz improvisation (p. 310).

37. Martin Buber, *I and Thou,* trans. Walter Kaufman (New York: Scribner's, 1970), p. 66.

38. Ralph Ellison, *Shadow and Act* (London: Secker and Warburg, 1964), p. 123.

39. Jahnheinz Jahn, *Muntu: The New African Culture* (New York: Grove, 1961), p. 223, as cited by Smith, *Conjuring Culture,* p. 123.

40. Myles Horton, *The Long Haul: An Autobiography* (New York: Anchor, 1990).

41. Toni Morrison evokes this sensibility in *Sula* (New York: Bantam, 1973) and in *Beloved* (New York: Knopf, 1987). Here we find a nondualistic language of good and evil, struggle and hope, which maintains the passion for justice without an illusion of ultimate victory, which acknowledges the persistent challenge of evil without resignation, nihilism, or cynicism. In *Sula,* the images are stark and compelling—evil is something to be endured, not defeated. In *Beloved,* the community that was complicitous in Sethe's tragedy returns to reclaim her, and this reclamation, while profound and healing, is itself partial. Sethe is reclaimed, Beloved is expelled, and yet the healing, for all its partiality, is a healing nonetheless, the matrix of further change, of life, of hope.

42. Muriel Rukeyser, "Fable," in *Collected Poems* (New York: McGraw-Hill, 1978), p. 554.

43. Karen McCarthy Brown, "Alourdes: A Case Study of Moral Leadership in Haitian Vodou," in *Saints and Virtues,* ed. John Hawley (Berkeley: University of California Press, 1987), p. 166.

44. Ibid., p. 166.

45. Ibid., p. 165.

46. Ibid., p. 167.

47. Ibid., p. 149.

48. Ibid., pp. 148–49.

49. Ibid., p. 150.

50. Ibid.

51. Ibid., p. 151.

52. Ibid.

53. Ibid., p. 154.

54. Ibid., pp. 153–54.

55. Ibid., p. 146.

56. Ibid., p. 160.

57. Ibid.

58. Ibid., p. 159.

59. Ibid., pp. 158–59.

60. Ibid., p. 161.

61. Ibid., p. 162.

62. Ibid., p. 165.

63. Ibid., p. 144.

64. Gerald Early, *Tuxedo Junction: Essays on American Culture* (New York: Echo Press, 1992), p. 229.

65. Peter Watrous, "Veteran Saxophonists," *New York Times,* April 15, 1996.

66. The Donatist controversy of fourth-century Christianity was multifaceted, but one dimension involved the validity of baptisms and ordinations performed by priests and bishops who were themselves thought to be unfaithful. For a fuller account, see Paul Johnson, *A History of Christianity* (New York: Atheneum, 1979), pp. 82–88, 113–20.

67. Mary Lou Williams as cited by Neil Leonard, *Jazz: Myth and Religion* (New York: Oxford University Press, 1987), p. 58.

68. Brown, "Alourdes," p. 144.

69. Kant, of course, raised four questions. I offer a postmodern exploration of the fourth, "what is man?," in chapters three and four.

CHAPTER 3

1. Robert Dole, as cited by B. Drummond Ayres Jr., "Dole Aims a Barrage at 'Intellectual Elites,'" *The New York Times,* September 5, 1995, p. A15.

2. Ibid.

3. Ibid.

4. Glenn C. Loury, *The New York Times Book Review,* "Across the Great Divide: New Calls for Understanding and Reconciliation from Two Venerable Warriors on Behalf of Racial Justice," June 23, 1996, p. 11.

5. Contrast Kanter's celebration of the possibilities of globalization with the indictment of persistent economic and political inequality by Davis, hooks, West, and

Bell. Rosabeth Moss Kanter, *World Class: Thriving Locally in the Global Economy* (New York: Simon and Schuster, 1995); Cornel West, *Race Matters* (New York: Vintage), 1994; Angela Y. Davis, *Women, Race and Class* (New York: Vintage Books, 1983); bell hooks, *Feminist Theory: From Margin to Center* (Boston: South End, 1984); bell hooks, *Talking Back: Thinking Feminist, Thinking Black* (Boston: South End, 1989); Derrick Bell, *Faces at the Bottom of the Well: The Permanence of Racism* (New York: Basic Books, 1992).

6. Margo Jefferson, "Sunday View: A Family's Story Merges with the Nations," *New York Times,* October 18, 1995, p. B-4.

7. Ellison as cited by Gerald Early, *Tuxedo Junction: Essays on American Culture* (New York: Echo Press, 1992), p. 289.

8. Patricia J. Williams, *The Alchemy of Race and Rights: Diary of a Law Professor* (Cambridge: Harvard University, 1991), p. 161.

9. Ibid., p. 158.

10. Ibid., p. 163.

11. Ibid., p. 165.

12. Ibid., pp. 164–65.

13. Muriel Rukeyser, *The Collected Poems of Muriel Rukeyser* (New York: McGraw-Hill, 1976), p. 475.

14. Audre Lorde, "Between Ourselves" *The Black Unicorn: Poems* (New York: W. W. Norton, 1978), p. 112.

15. Fraser, *Justice Interruptus: Critical Reflections on the "Postsocialist" Condition* (New York: Routledge, 1997), pp. 1–3.

16. Ibid., p. 2.

17. Ibid.

18. See for example Bonnano's and Constance's discussion of the economic disruption caused by progressive attempts to protect dolphins from tuna fishing. Alessandro Bonanno and Douglas Constance, *Caught in the Net: The Global Tuna Industry, Environmentalism, and the State* (Lawrence, KS: University Press of Kansas, 1996).

19. Williams, *The Alchemy of Race and Rights,* p. 173.

20. See Janet Jakobson's examination of relativism in *Working Alliances and the Politics of Difference: Diversity in Feminist Ethics* (Bloomington: Indiana University Press, forthcoming).

21. Alasdair McIntryre, *After Virtue: A Study in Moral Theory,* 2d ed. (Notre Dame, IN: University of Notre Dame Press, 1984).

22. Ibid.

23. Ibid.

24. Michel Foucault, *The Archaeology of Knowledge and the Discourse on Language* (New York: Harper and Row, 1972), pp. 215–37.

25. I explore this issue in more detail in Sharon Welch, *A Feminist Ethic of Risk* (Minneapolis, MN: Fortress, 1989), p. 126.

26. Lillian Smith, *Killers of the Dream* (New York: W. W. Norton, 1994), pp. 25–26.

27. Ibid., p. 27.

28. Ibid., pp. 28–29.

29. Margaret Rose Gladney, introduction to Smith, *Killers of the Dream,* unpaginated. If paginated, would be pp. ii–iii.

30. Richard Barnet, *The Roots of War: The Men and Institutions Behind U.S. Foreign Policy* (New York: Penguin, 1971).

31. Ibid., ch. 3.

32. Ibid., pp. 119–20.

33. Joseph A. Maxwell, "Diversity, Solidarity, and Community," forthcoming, *Educational Review*: 1.

34. Fullinwider, as cited by Maxwell, "Diversity," p. 1.

35. Richard Rorty, as cited by Maxwell, "Diversity."

36. Maxwell, "Diversity," p.4.

37. Ibid., pp. 6–7.

38. Clifford Geertz, as cited by Maxwell, "Diversity," pp. 9–10.

39. Maxwell, "Diversity," p.11.

40. Ibid.

41. Ibid.

42. Jane Smiley, *Moo: A Novel* (New York: Fawcett Columbine, 1995), p. 193.

43. This form of community identity has affinities with Mary Daly's definition of the soul. Rather than focusing on the "soul" as a stable or fixed essence, she describes it as a "telic focusing and metapatterning principle" (pp. 352–53). Daly claims that our "essences" are changing, based on a passionate connection with other beings who are also in flux "constantly unfolding, creating, communicating—Be-ing more" (p. 30). Mary Daly, *Pure Lust: Elemental Feminist Philosophy* (Boston: Beacon, 1984).

44. Lynda Stone, ed., *Education Feminism Reader* (New York: Routledge, 1994).

45. Karen Baker-Fletcher also described her teaching in these terms in a discussion at the American Academy of Religion, November 1996, New Orleans, Louisiana.

46. Barbara Ehrenreich, *The Hearts of Men: American Dreams and the Flight from Commitment* (Garden City, NY: Anchor Press/Doubleday, 1983); and Paula M. Cooey, *Family, Freedom and Faith: Building Community Today* (Louisville, KY: Westminster John Knox, 1996).

47. Christine Sleeter and Carl A. Grant, *Making Choices for Multicultural Education* (New York: Merrill, 1994).

48. Ibid., ch. 2, pp. 41–42.

49. Ibid., ch. 3, pp. 85–89.

50. Ibid., ch. 4, pp. 123–26.

51. Ibid., ch. 5, pp. 167–69.

52. Ibid., ch. 6, pp. 209–12.

53. Ibid., ch. 2, pp. 44–52.

54. Ibid., pp. 52–58.

55. Ibid., pp. 58–61.

56. Ibid., pp. 72–79.

57. Ibid.

58. Ibid., ch. 3, pp. 85–89.

59. Ibid., pp. 95–98.

60. Ibid., pp. 89–95.

61. Ibid., pp. 95–100, 102–06.

62. Ibid., pp. 106–09.

63. Ibid., pp. 109–10.

64. Ibid., pp. 110–12.

65. Ibid., pp. 114–18.

66. Ibid., p. 118.

67. Ibid.

68. Ibid., ch. 4, pp. 123–26.

69. Ibid.,pp. 126–33.

70. Ibid., pp. 139–41, 144–47.

71. Iris Marion Young, *Justice and the Politics of Difference* (Princeton: Princeton University Press, 1990).

72. Sleeter and Grant, *Making Choices for Multicultural Education,* ch. 4.

73. Ibid., ch. 5, pp. 167–73.

74. Ibid., ch. 6, pp. 209–12.

75. Ibid., pp. 223–30.

76. For a complex description of African American life see Marcia Riggs, *Awake, Arise and Act: A Womanist Call for Black Liberation* (Cleveland, OH: Pilgrim Press, 1994); Karen Baker-Fletcher and Garth Kasimu Baker-Fletcher, *My Sister My Brother: Womanist and Xodus God-Talk* (Maryknoll, NY: Orbis Books, 1997).

77. Susan Thistlethewaite, *Sex, Race and God: Christian Feminism in Black and White* (New York: Crossroad, 1989); Ruth Frankenberg, *White Women, Race Matters: The Social Construction of Whiteness* (Minneapolis, MN: University of Minnesota, 1993).

78. Cherrie Moraga and Gloria Anzaldua, eds., *This Bridge Called My Back: Writings by Radical Women of Color* (Watertown, MA: Persephone, 1981); Gloria Anzaldua, ed., *Making Face, Making Soul* (San Francisco: Spinsters, 1990).

CHAPTER 4

1. Nelle Morton, *The Journey Is Home* (Boston: Beacon, 1985).

2. Papusa Molina, "Recognizing, Accepting, and Celebrating Our Differences," in *Making Face, Making Soul,* ed. Gloria Anzaldua (San Francisco: Spinsters, 1990); Sara Lucia Hoagland, *Lesbian Ethics: Toward New Value* (Palo Alto, CA: Institute of Lesbian Studies, 1988).

3. bell hooks, "Feminism and Racism: The Struggle Continues," *Z Magazine* (July/August 1990), p.41.

4. For a thorough examination of the theoretical issues involved in a postmodern understanding of democracy and the role of education in enabling liberating citizenship, see Peter McLaren and Henry A. Giroux, "Writing from the Margins: Geographies of Identity, Pedagogy, and Power" in Peter McLaren, *Revolutionary Multiculturalism: Pedagogies of Dissent for the New Millennium* (Boulder, CO: Westview, 1997), pp. 16-41, and Henry A. Giroux, *Living Dangerously: Multiculturalism and the Politics of Difference* (New York: Peter Lang, 1993). Rebecca Chopp also acknowledges the complexity of democracy as a process and discusses the role of public theology in general and a feminist, Christian, prophetic pragmatism in particular in maintaining a non-patriarchal democracy "constituted through narratives, practices and visions of multiculturalism" (p. 112). She also address the tensions in democracy, and points to the need for a change in "fundamental attitudes:" "Americans, as the authors of the recent volume *The Good Society* suggest, have a fundamental attitude of fear and need to move to one of trust and, I would add, openness. But where are sources for trust? One place is the emergent tradition of prophetic pragmatism, which combines a reading of Christian tradition in which an attitude of fundamental trust replaces the fear invoked and sustained in patriarchal monotheism. And certainly, feminist theology is greatly concerned to create a certain type of openness to the world, one that does not negate the self but opens the self to encounters with those who are different. Such concern for new narratives of women's lives is matched, in feminist theology, with the concern for new practices and visions of community" (p. 128). Rebecca S. Chopp, "A Feminist Perspective: Christianity, Democracy, and Feminist Theology," in *Christianity and Democracy in a Global Context,* ed. John Witte, Jr. (Boulder, CO: Westview, 1993), pp. 111-29.

5. The Equity Institute, formerly based in California, provided diversity training for businesses, colleges, non-profit organizations, and social change organizations.

6. Carol Lee Sanchez, *Excerpts from a Mountain Climber's Handbook: Selected Poems, 1971-1984* (San Francisco: Taurean Horn, 1985), p. 18.

7. Aristotle, *The Ethics of Aristotle,* trans. J. A. K. Thomson (Baltimore, MD: Penguin, 1953).

8. Michel Foucault, *The Use of Pleasure: The History of Sexuality, vol. II* (New York: Pantheon Books, 1985), p. 22.

9. Ibid, p. 80.

10. Ibid, p. 70.

11. Ibid., p. 75.

12. Sanchez, *Excerpts from a Mountain Climber's Handbook,* p. 3.

13. Ibid., pp. 4–5.

14. Thomas Berry, *Dreams of the Earth* (San Francisco: Sierra Club Books, 1988).

15. Carol Lee Sanchez, "Animal, Vegetable, and Mineral: The Sacred Connection," in *Ecofeminism and the Sacred,* ed. Carol J. Adams (New York: Continuum, 1993).

16. Peter Applebome, "Crime Fear Is Seen Forcing Changes in Youth Behavior," *New York Times,* January 12, 1996, p. A6.

17. Ibid.

18. Stanley Crouch, "Who Are We? Where Did We Come From? Where Are We Going?" in *Lure and Loathing,* ed. Gerald Early (New York: Penguin, 1993), p. 82.

19. Rosemary Radford Ruether, "Women and Culture," *Conscience* (Winter 1995/96), p. 13.

20. Ibid, p.15.

21. Michel Foucault, "The Political Technology of Individuals," in *Technologies of the Self: A Seminar with Michel Foucault,* ed. L. H. Martin, H. Guttman, P. H. Hutton (Amherst, MA: University of Massachusetts, 1988), p. 146.

22. Foucault, "Political Technology of Individuals," p. 15.

23. Ibid., p. 11.

24. Ibid., p. 10.

25. For a discussion of the interaction of feminist and postmodern theory in critical pedagogy, see Henry A. Giroux, ed. *Postmodernism, Feminism, and Cultural Politics* (Albany, New York: SUNY, 1991).

26. Peter McLaren, *Schooling as a Ritual Performance: Towards a Political Economy of Educational Symbols and Gestures* (London and New York: Routledge, 1994); Henry A. Giroux, *Disturbing Pleasures: Learning Popular Culture* (New York: Routledge, 1994), pp.141–52.

27. David R. Dickens, "Postmodernism and Interactionist Thought," in *Wilderness of Mirrors: Symbolic Interactionism and Postmodernism,* ed. Jonathan Epstein (New York: Garland Press, forthcoming), p. 6.

28. David R. Dickens, "Postmodernism, Cultural Studies and Contemporary Social Inquiry," in *Cultural Studies,* Vol. 1 (1995), p.3.

29. David R. Roediger, *The Wages of Whiteness: Race and the Making of the American Working Class* (London: Verso, 1991); Cornel West, *Prophesy Deliverance! An Afro-American Revolutionary Christianity* (Philadelphia: Westminster, 1982); Peter McLaren, "Unthinking Whiteness, Rethinking Democracy: Critical Citizenship in Gringolandia," in McLaren, *Revolutionary Multiculturalism,* pp. 237–93; Henry A. Giroux, "Living Dangerously: Identity Politics and the New Cultural Racism—Towards a Critical Pedagogy of Representation," in Giroux, *Living Dangerously,* pp. 89–124.

30. Emilie M.Townes, *In a Blaze of Glory: Womanist Spirituality as Social Witness* (Nashville: Abingdon, 1995), p. 49.

31. Ibid., pp. 49–50.

32. Ibid., p. 50.

33. Ibid., p. 66.

34. Ibid., p. 65.

35. Ibid., p.68.

36. Dickens, citing Stuart Hall in "Postmodernism, Cultural Studies and Contemporary Social Inquiry," pp. 9–10.

37. Sanchez, "Animal, Vegetable, and Mineral," p. 226.

38. Ibid.

39. Ibid., pp. 226–27.

40. Iris Marion Young, for example, states that it is important to "distinguish between blaming people and holding them responsible." "Blame is a backward-looking concept. Calling on agents to take responsibility for their actions, habits, feelings, attitudes, images, and associations, on the other hand, is forward-looking; it asks the person 'from here on out' to submit such unconscious behavior to reflection, to work to change habits and attitudes." Iris Marion Young, *Justice and the Politics of Difference* (Princeton, NJ: Princeton University Press, 1990), p.151.

41. A critique of this approach to racial justice, and the formulation of an alternative approach focusing on responsibility but not blame, has been developed through work on racial justice initiatives with the following members of the Unitarian Universalist Association: Anita Farber-Robertson, Thandeka, Lola Peters, Mark Morrison-Reed, Jean Kapuscik, William Jones, Michelle Bentley, and Marjorie Bowens-Wheatley. This approach has also been developed through work with diversity training teams at the University of Missouri and conversations with Diane Williams, KC Morrison, Mable Grimes, and Karen Touzeau.

42 Judith H. Katz, "The Sociopolitical Nature of Counseling," *The Counseling Psychologist* 13 (4) 1985, p. 618.

43. James Luther Adams, *The Prophethood of All Believers,* ed. George K. Beach (Boston: Beacon, 1986), ch. 2.

44. Roediger's analysis of the genesis of the category of whiteness not only is accurate, but also needs to be held in creative tension with other dimensions of the culture of white Americans, values and structures that have led to resistance to racism and other forms of injustice.

45. Molly Ivins, *Molly Ivins Can't Say That, Can She?* (New York: Random House, 1991), p. 18.

46. Stephen B. Boyd, W. Merle Longwood, and Mark W. Muesse, eds. *Redeeming Men: Religion and Masculinities* (Louisville, KY: Westminster John Knox, 1996).

47. Starhawk, in *Women Respond to the Men's Movement: A Feminist Collection,* ed. Kay Leigh Hagan (San Francisco: HarperCollins, 1992), p. 29.

48. Vivian Gussin Paley, *Kwanzaa and Me: A Teacher's Story* (Cambridge: Harvard University Press, 1995).

49. Ibid., p. 67.

50. I learned this exercise from two sources: the work of Thandeka, who derives from it a complex and compelling account of white racial identity and the implications of that identity formation for work for racial justice; and from the Equity Institute. Trainers at Equity also used the exercise of first memories of sexual and class identity.

51. Dr. William Jones, presentation of the "Grid of Oppression," University of Missouri-Columbia (October 1992).

52. Andrew Hacker, *Two Nations Black and White, Separate, Hostile, Unequal* (New York: Charles Scribner's Sons, 1992); Angela Y. Davis, *Women, Race, and Class* (New York: Vintage, 1983); Barbara Ehrenreich, *Fear of Falling: The Inner Life of the Middle Class* (New York: HarperCollins, 1990).

53. This analysis of agents, allies, empowered and targeted groups is based on the model developed by Equity Institute, and as practiced by the diversity training teams at the University of Missouri. For a description of these categories see Joan Steinau Lester, *The Future of White Men and Other Diversity Dilemmas* (Berkeley, CA: Conari Press, 1994), pp. 95–110.

54. Rosabeth Moss Kanter, *Men and Women of the Corporation* (New York: Basic, 1977) and Leola Johnson, "Black Caucuses and Women's Caucuses in the Newsroom," lecture at the University of Missouri, Columbia, MO, March 1993.

55. Kanter, *Women and Men,* ch. 8.

56. Ibid.

57. Ibid.

58. Michael Bader, "Fear of Success," in *Tikkun* (Spring 1997).

59. Studs Terkel, introduction to Virginia Foster Durr, *Outside the Magic Circle,* ed. Hollinger F. Barnard (Tuscaloosa, AL: The University of Alabama Press, 1985).

CHAPTER 5

1. Jacques Derrida, "Racism's Last Word," *Critical Inquiry* 12.1 (1985), pp. 290–99. Nancy Fraser describes a 1980 conference in which the participants explored the political implications of Derrida's work and focused on the role of the aesthetic in his thought. Many of the followers of Derrida expressed a strong "suspicion of the political, thereby seeming to surrender the possibility of political opposition to administration and instrumental reason." No wonder, then, that some members concluded that henceforth such opposition must be waged under the banner of "the ethical or the aesthetic, even the religious." Nancy Fraser, *Unruly Practices: Power, Discourse and Gender in Contemporary Social Theory* (Minneapolis: University of Minnesota Press, 1989), p. 90.

2. Emil Fackenheim, *To Mend the World: Foundations of Future Jewish Thought* (New York: Schocken, 1982), p. 235.

3. David R. Gushee, *The Righteous Gentiles of the Holocaust: A Christian Interpretation* (Minneapolis, MN: Fortress, 1994), ch. 2–3.

4. Christopher Browning, *Ordinary Men: Reserve Police Battalion 101 and the Final Solution in Poland* (New York: Harper, 1992).

5. J. Alan Moore, "Browning's Ordinary Men: Evil and Remorse," Unpublished essay (April 1995), p. 4.

6. See also Daniel Goldhagen, *Hitler's Willing Executioners: Ordinary Germans and the Holocaust* (New York: Knopf, 1996).

7. Fackenheim, *To Mend the World*, p. 235.

8. E. Bernard Bethge, *Bonhoeffer, Exile and Martyr*, ed. John W. deGruchy (London: Collins, 1975).

9. Paul Johnson, *A History of Christianity* (New York: Atheneum, 1979), pp. 481–94.

10. Gushee, *The Righteous Gentiles of the Holocaust*, chaps. 2–3.

11. Bonhoeffer, "History and Good," in *Ethics*, ed. Eberhard Bethge (New York: Macmillan, 1955), ch. 6.

12. Ibid., pp. 240–62.

13. Ibid.

14. Ibid.

15. Ibid., pp. 261–62. Bonhoeffer described what was entailed in accepting ambiguity as follows: "A breach of the law must be recognized in all its gravity.... Whether an action arises from responsibility or from cynicism is shown only by whether or not the objective guilt of the violation of the law is recognized and acknowledged, and by whether or not, precisely in this violation, the law is hallowed." Bonhoeffer, *Ethics*, pp. 261–62.

16. Jane Flax, "The End Of Innocence," in *Feminists Theorize the Political*, ed. Judith Butler and Joan W. Scott (New York: Routledge, 1992), pp. 459–60.

17. María Lugones argues that it is the inability to see ourselves as we are seen by women of color that prevents white feminists from fully understanding difference and ambiguity, and the centrality of difference and ambiguity in any "creative strategy of resistance" (p. 43): "It is not that we are the only faithful mirrors, but I think we are faithful mirrors. Not that we show you as you really are; we just show you as one of the people that you are. What we reveal to you is that you are many—something that may in itself be frightening to you. But the self we reveal to you is also one that you are not eager to know for reasons that one may conjecture (p. 42)." The self revealed to white women by women of color is a self that denies women of color substance, credibility, an appropriate degree of authority (neither too much nor too little), and independence despite our "good" intentions (p. 43). María C. Lugones, "On the Logic of Pluralist Feminism" in *Feminist Ethics*, ed. Claudia Card (Lawrence, KS: University of Kansas, 1991).

18. Simone Schwarz-Bart, *The Bridge of Beyond* (Oxford: Heinemann, 1982), p. 31.

19. Ibid., p. 51.

20. Ralph Ellison, *Shadow and Act* (London: Secker and Warburg, 1967), pp. 78-79.

21. Gerald Early, *Tuxedo Junction: Essays on American Culture* (New York: Ecco, 1992), pp. 109–10.

22. Ralph Ellison, *Shadow and Act,* p. 256.

23. Freda Dröes provides a thought-provoking definition of religion in her analysis of the photography of Cindy Sherman. She points to two definitions of religion. The first is the most well known and is the definition I am using. Here "religion is thought to derive from the Latin verb 'religare' and means to bind together, to connect." I argue that in spirituality this "binding together" is both ecstatic and amoral. Dröes points to another definition of religion. If religion stems from the Latin verb "relegere," "religion takes on the meaning of 'examine again, consider repeatedly, observe.' This too may be interpreted in a positive and negative way.... The first definition can be subsumed under the notion of 'the giving of meaning.' The other interpretation can be understood as 'the developing of conscience.'" Freda Dröes, "Sherman's Shadows" in *Begin with the Body: Corporeality Religion and Gender,* ed. Jonneke Bekkenkamp and Maaike de Haardt (Leuven, the Netherlands: Peeters, 1998), p. 113. This latter aspect of religion is like that described by Carol Lee Sanchez.

24. Friedrich Nietzsche, *Beyond Good and Evil: Prelude to a Philosophy of the Future,* trans. Walter Kaufmann (New York: Vintage, 1966).

25. For a discussion of both the ways in which irony and religiosity are at odds with one another, and the dangers of religiosity without irony, see Jonneke Bekkenkamp, "Breaking the Waves: Corporality and Religion in a Modern Melodrama" in *Begin with the Body,* pp. 134–56. In contrast to Catherine Bates' claim that there is "no sin but irony," Bekkenkamp argues for the value of irony, while still claiming that overcoming irony is necessary for "involvement and receptiveness" (p. 156). I am arguing, however, that using the jazz aesthetic as a model for ethical and political engagement allows us to be ironic and committed to justice, suspicious and celebrative of moments of joy and healing.

26. Zygmunt Bauman, *Postmodern Ethics* (Oxford: Basil Blackwell, 1993), p.73.

27. Ibid., pp. 88–92.

28. Ibid., p. 80.

29. Ibid., p. 88.

30. Ibid., pp. 91–92.

31. For a critique of this definition of caring, see Alice Miller, *For Your Own Good: Hidden Cruelty in Child-Rearing and the Roots of Violence* (New York: Farrar Strauss Giroux, 1983).

32. Hoagland acknowledges both the importance of caring in ethical action, and the limitations of this concept. She argues that it reflects "the heterosexual model of feminine virtues"—"self-sacrifice, vulnerability, and altruism" (p. 246). She points to the intrinsic limits of an understanding of caring based on the mother-child bond: such

an ethic ignores the ambiguity and evil present in that bond (resentment and, at times, abuse), it is inadequate to the challenges of care between equals, inadequate to the challenges of responsibility for those who are distant, and it is inadequate to the challenges of responsibility in the face of structural barriers such as racism. Sarah Lucia Hoagland, "Some Thoughts About Caring," in *Feminist Ethics,* ed. Claudia Card (Lawrence, KS: University of Kansas, 1991), pp. 246–63. See also Kathryn Tanner's critical review of the feminist ethic of care and the challenges of combining care and justice. Kathryn Tanner, "The Care That Does Justice: recent writings in feminist ethics and theology," *Journal of Religious Ethics,* Spring 1996, v. 24.1, pp. 171–91.

33. Betty Friedan, *The Feminine Mystique* (New York: Dell, 1963); Sara Evans, *Personal Politics: The Roots of Women's Liberation in the Civil Rights Movement and the New Left* (New York: Knopf, 1978).

34. Marie Fortune, *Sexual Violence: The Unmentionable Sin, an Ethical and Pastoral Perspective* (New York: Pilgrim, 1983).

35. See Patricia Hill Collins, *Black Feminist Thought: Knowledge, Consciousness and Politics* (New York: Routledge, 1991).

36. See Marianne Hirsch and Evelyn Fox Keller, eds., *Conflicts in Feminism* (New York: Routledge, 1990).

37. For a thorough analysis of mutuality and interdependence, see Judith V. Jordan, Alexandra G. Kaplan, Jean Baker Miller, Irene P. Stiver, and Janet L. Surrey, *Women's Growth in Connection: Writings from the Stone Center* (New York: Guildford Press, 1991).

38. Bauman, *Postmodern Ethics,* p. 52.

39. Ibid., p. 92.

40. Ibid., ch. 3.

41. See the study of long-term commitment to social justice by Sharon Daloz Parks, Larry Parks Daloz, Cheryl H. Keen, and James P. Keen, *Common Fire: Lives of Commitment in a Complex World* (Boston: Beacon, 1996).

42. Morris Miller, "The Chicken-Little Syndrome and Its Implications," working paper, June 1995, p. 3.

43. Michel Foucault, "Nietzsche, Genealogy and History," in *Language, Counter-memory and Practice,* ed. Donald F. Bouchard (Ithaca, NY: Cornell University Press, 1977), p. 143.

44. Molly Ivins, *Nothin' But Good Times Ahead* (New York: Vintage, 1994), pp. 113–14.

45. Ibid., p. 252.

46. Catherine Keller, *Apocalypse Now and Then: A Feminist Guide to the End of the World* (Boston: Beacon, 1996), p. 30, makes a similar claim: "To stand in some particular fragility of place and time, with one's fragments of community and materiali ties of gender, and to love life: that is perhaps the only real basis of action against the end of the world."

INDEX